Steve —

Thanks for your

Understanding Economic Equilibrium

Support + especially

for your friendship

over the years!

Mike

Understanding Economic Equilibrium

Making Your Way Through an Interdependent World

Thomas J. Cunningham and Mike Shaw

BUSINESS EXPERT PRESS

Leader in applied, concise business books

Understanding Economic Equilibrium:
Making Your Way Through an Interdependent World

Copyright © Business Expert Press, LLC, 2021.

Cover design by Cindy Beebe Langley

Interior design by Exeter Premedia Services Private Ltd., Chennai, India

First published in 2021 by
Business Expert Press, LLC
222 East 46th Street, New York, NY 10017
www.businessexpertpress.com

ISBN-13: 978-1-63742-038-6 (paperback)
ISBN-13: 978-1-63742-039-3 (e-book)

Business Expert Press Economics and Public Policy Collection

Collection ISSN: 2163-761X (print)
Collection ISSN: 2163-7628 (electronic)

First edition: 2021

10 9 8 7 6 5 4 3 2 1

Description

Economic agents all over the world are trying to maximize their returns given their efforts, resources, and opportunities. They come together in markets that ultimately allocate goods and services among many competing interests. We can readily see how individual markets behave; it's more difficult, but exponentially more important, to recognize the general equilibrium across all markets. Disturbances in one market have implications for others.

These interrelationships are particularly important to understand when policy changes are being considered where actions in one market will impose changes on other markets, and not always in obvious or pleasant ways. *Understanding Economic Equilibrium* reveals how all markets fit together, and how we as individuals fit into that bigger picture.

Keywords

economics; the economy; global economy; economists; GDP; gross domestic product; goods and services; equilibrium; macroeconomics; macroeconomy; free trade; supply and demand; Federal Reserve; the Fed; consumers and consumption; productivity and wages; labor markets; inflation; national income accounts; investment and inventories

Contents

Preface

This book was a joint effort, in the truest sense of the words, between myself and my coauthor, Tom Cunningham. Throughout our four-year acquaintance I found his ideas inspiring and he found my ability to communicate them a compliment to those ideas. I was delighted when he agreed to my suggestion that we write a book together. We were looking forward to its publication and planned to celebrate the event as one would expect coauthors to do. Unfortunately, on December 27, 2020, Tom died unexpectedly, approximately five months before the book was scheduled to be published. While I am delighted that our book is now available, the occasion of its publication is bittersweet without Tom here to enjoy it with me.

I first met Tom Cunningham in the spring of 2016 at a national banking conference sponsored by a client we shared. I was covering the presentations, writing summaries for a digest the client emailed each year following the conference to about 5,000 bankers. Presenters included senior-level advisors from leading national accounting firms, federal regulators, association officials, and members of the Financial Accounting Standards Board, which had just released a new accounting standard designed to prevent the kind of institutional stress and outright failures generated by the Great Recession.

The conference was in its fifth year and had developed a reputation as substantive and important, especially now that the attendees were going to be responsible for determining their banks' quarterly reserves based on the new and complicated accounting standard. It was Tom's first year to speak at the conference, his role as a recently retired Federal Reserve Bank senior economist to provide somewhat of a break from all the accounting speak with a summary view of the status of the U.S. economy. And while the audience was entertained with tidbits like his explanation of economics as "the dismal science," they were stilled by his understanding of the workings of the world's economies, insights amassed over thirty years researching macroeconomic realities and developing rationale for U.S. economic policy.

When the conference concluded and speaker ratings were compiled, Tom was the highest rated of the presenters, including two individuals who helped write the new standard. He had captivated his audience with a delivery as entertaining as it was informative, as clear and decipherable as it was insightful. Off stage, following his presentation and at the conference dinners and socials, he was swarmed by attendees with questions from how Brexit would affect the U.S. economy to how the markets would perform in the coming year, why inflation was low, and how baby boomers aging out of the labor force would impact GDP. And no matter how short his drink or cold his dinner, no question went unanswered.

Our mutual client was no dummy. The client knew Tom's appeal and celebrity with this group of bankers was something to capitalize on more than once a year. Tom and I had become something of conference pals, as well as coconspirators as I was the one committing his spoken words to the written word. And when the client asked him to write a monthly blog, Tom invited me to work with him as his editor. We co-wrote the blog the first Friday morning of each month as the Bureau of Labor Statistics released its employment report until the client sold the business to a consolidator at the end of 2017. The new owners wisely kept Tom and his blog on board, but assigned the editing to their in-house writers.

But I'm no dummy either. I'd been writing about financial issues for financial businesses for more than forty years, long enough to recognize how uniquely Tom connected with audiences, how much he could convey in a few easily digestible sentences, how easy he made it to understand why money makes the world go 'round.

It was August 2019 and the first time I'd talked with Tom since our client had been acquired. "Hi, Tom. It's Mike Shaw. Have you ever thought about writing a book?" Of course he hadn't. With almost weekly speaking engagements and now as chief economist for the Atlanta Chamber of Commerce, when would he find time? Hell, he didn't even have a website. But the more I pressed the better the idea must have sounded, because I was able to convince him to give it a try.

Getting a business book published starts with writing a proposal that includes sample chapters and a detailed outline and is carefully formatted according to the directions in one of the plethora of books telling you how to write a business book proposal. (Writing a book about how to get published is one of the surest ways to get published.) It took Tom and I almost a year to complete our proposal, but when we submitted it for consideration, it elicited interest, including from the publisher for whom we are now so grateful.

What you will read here is absolutely consistent with how Tom talked to his audiences. He explained in plain language the key ingredients in the global economic soup, simplifying what can be difficult concepts complicated by the intricacies of how they work with and against each other, how they interconnect and interrelate. What's the difference between real and nominal GDP? How do global financial markets determine the value of a publicly traded U.S. manufacturer? What does it mean to "pay the losers" and why does it make sense? And what is an inverted yield curve actually telling us?

Tom called it the equilibrium principle, and how that unfolds, what it means to our daily economic existences as well as the U.S. and world economies, is what to look for and forward to in these pages.

Thank you, Tom.

Mike Shaw

Acknowledgement

We are grateful for the contributions of Dr. Rosemary Cunningham, economist, professor, and Tom's wife, who stepped in to fill the expertise gap after her husband's untimely death. She helped us through the final editing and continues to be involved with the project, providing supplemental teaching materials and ongoing marketing support.

PART I

The Equilibrium Principle: A Natural Dynamic State

CHAPTER 1

What Happens There Matters Here

To contemporize the oft-employed James Carville quip, "It's the *global* economy, stupid."

- When China imposed retaliatory tariffs on soybean imports from American farmers, sales at Iowa's department stores declined along with farm family incomes.
- Brexit could disrupt Northern Ireland's dairy industry, forcing it to market its cheese and butter globally, as the Republic of Ireland might no longer have free-trade access to Northern Irish milk.
- A bargain price for a lakefront lot in Alexander City, Alabama, could bring capital into the United States from a buyer in Alexandria, Egypt.
- The outbreak of the COVID-19 virus in Wuhan, China, led not only to a worldwide pandemic but to a worldwide economic crisis.

As the world grows smaller, an economic shift in one nation increasingly impacts the rest of the world. We now live and work in a global economy—and less than three decades since the Clinton campaign slogan that virtually no one, including the campaign, thought applied to anything but one country.

The economy is in a continuous, dynamic equilibrium, an interaction of competing interests: those who supply and those who demand a good or service. Equilibrium is at work in all markets and all societies—and the complex interactions are not always apparent.

Most of us get our economic education in small, discrete pieces from disparate newsfeeds. Tariffs are hurting Midwestern farmers. Inflation is out of control in Venezuela. A strike by Eastern Kentucky coalminers doesn't seem relevant to a couple in Georgia budgeting their monthly expenses. But it is. We are part of a larger system, the particulars of which aren't always apparent.

If you were a soybean farmer in the Midwest, those Chinese tariffs might have ushered you into bankruptcy. But if you owned a dress shop in a farm state, you suffered as well, because the farmer's family didn't have money to spend on new clothes. On the other hand, a New York City restaurateur benefited as lower prices for soybeans drove down the costs of raising chicken and beef and the restaurant's costs to produce its signature dishes.

The COVID-19 virus lockdown of a meat packing plant in Idaho created a shortage of pork in the grocery stores in North Carolina, while farmers euthanized pigs. Hospitals overcrowded with COVID-19 patients suffered financial losses because they couldn't perform elective surgeries.

A partial equilibrium view of things can be misleading. Take minimum wage policy, for example. Raising the minimum wage seems like a good way to increase the incomes of the working poor. But some employers might not be able to afford to increase their workers' wages, so jobs are lost. On the other hand, higher wages would likely result in increased spending, which leads to more employment. As we will see in the chapter "Wages: Minimum and More," an analysis of minimum-wage changes shows mixed and complex results.

In defining how local as well as global economies work, the principle of equilibrium explains both the mundane, like the price of chickens and the rise in mortgage rates, and the more esoteric, like mushrooming health care costs and an ever-rising national debt. *Understanding Economic Equilibrium* examines both the particular and the broad, providing information and insight on how the world's economies work together, information and insight you can use to improve how your economy works for you.

Takeaways

- The economy is in a continuous, dynamic equilibrium, an interaction of competing interests: those who supply and those who demand a good or service.
- A partial equilibrium view of things can be misleading.
- In defining how local as well as global economies work, the principle of equilibrium explains both the mundane and the esoteric.

CHAPTER 2

It's the *Global* Economy

We know that a nation is better off when it interacts with another nation with different economic strengths and weaknesses. It's a matter of comparative advantage. We do better doing what we're better at doing compared to the country we're trading with. The United States can't compete with Costa Rica on growing bananas, but we do have a comparative advantage making cars. So we sell them cars and buy their bananas.

Long ago, Marco Polo and the Silk Road proved the point by commingling the interests of Chinese textile producers, Middle East and European merchants, and wealthy Europeans and their tastes for East Asian spices and fine Chinese silks. You could make a lot of money if you were an industrious trader with a ship sailing between Europe and China and to the exotic locations along the Silk Road where you could find those spices. Those spices were, in fact, the first drivers of trade, and the industry seeking them out, the genesis of a first pass at a global economy.

Commerce in general emerged in the Middle East because it was centrally located for travel throughout the Eurasian land mass. People of different nations began interacting with each other economically, and found themselves better off as a result of it. Technical innovations ensued, leading to more and more trading opportunities. Advances in finance, accounting, sailing and logistics—all technologies that we now take for granted that had to be invented to take advantage of the benefits of inter-nation trading. Double-entry bookkeeping, introduced to the world in the late fifteenth century in Milan, Italy, by Leonardo da Vinci's math teacher Luca Pacioli, was an important contribution to global trade. (It just wasn't possible to keep track of multiple trading relationships with multiple trading partners in different locations via single-entry bookkeeping.) As well, checks were invented in Basra, Iraq, in the early eleventh century as a primitive banking tool that allowed you to complete a deal without having all the money in your pocket or stashed away in a chest toted by your caravan. The profits from trade generated thousands of innovations to facilitate more trade, a cycle that continues to this day.

North American Industrialization

While the U.S. participation in the colonial trading system was largely driven by England, other colonial powers were interested in what they found here. The new nation was rich in resources and a willing citizenry, entrepreneurial in spirit and eager to build wealth. Beginning around the time of the Civil War and extending through the 1940s, the United States grew into a major player in the world economy. While some European powers were looking elsewhere—Germany was courting Argentina and its neighbors in the Southern Cone—an industrialized United States emerged as the super economic power, the world's largest economy, by the end of World War II.

Technology is fungible, fairly easily transferred across spaces. Other nations recognized how industrialization had set up the United States and parts of Europe to become economic forces and moved in the same direction, capitalizing on their own advantages, like cheap labor, to capture manufacturing business. That didn't rob the United States of manufacturing capacity; the rest of the world picked up on the technology that had been developed in the United States and Europe, and by emulating much of what happened in those countries, emerging economies generated their own economic growth spurts. That has made the United States an increasingly smaller part of the global economy, not because of a defect here, but because the rest of the world is figuring it out.

Emerging Economies

The United States is home to only about 5 percent of the world's population, so the idea that we'll continue as the biggest economy on the planet isn't viable as countries with larger populations adopt more productive technologies. China and India each have more than four times the U.S. population, meaning either would need only one-fourth the per capita income of the United States to be a bigger economy. Over time, as nations adopt more productive technologies, their economies should be expected to rank more or less in relation to their populations. So the United States might fall comparatively but not in amount of productivity and certainly not in capability.

An emerging economy can adopt what a first-world economy would consider outdated technology, do so relatively cheaply, and get tremendous productivity gains. Not only is the old technology cheaper than leading-edge innovation, it is well understood, which lowers the cost of implementation. Emerging economies are now centers of growth, and since many are starting from such a low base, we should expect their percentage growth rates to be relatively high for a long time. On the other hand, the United States is the world's technology leader; development here is about innovation and pushing the envelope, not about adopting somebody else's advances.

That other economies are catching up in terms of per capita income is not something we should fear. Consider Monaco. That nation would dominate the world economy on a per capita income basis, but they're small. The United States remains both large and productive; we just don't have as many people as some emerging economies.

Disruptions to Trade

All this progress was paused, the unrelenting pace of economic growth in developed as well as emerging nations stalled, by a global pandemic that struck in early 2020. Europe initially contained the COVID-19 virus better than the United States, but in the process, it shut down a substantial portion of the world's supply chain. Other emerging economies faced the same problem, and the global supply chain was severely compromised, posing a major challenge to getting things everywhere started again. Then a second wave of the pandemic—perhaps it was only a continuation of the initial wave—swept through Europe and the United States and through virtually every one of the world's 195 countries. Restoring trade relationships and global supply chains will be challenging as different societies recover at different paces.

Boeing's Max 737 production shutdown illuminates the state of interaction and interdependency among economies and how a single event can affect so many. Boeing is a multinational corporation and made it a point to buy materials and parts for the airliner from countries where they do business, which is most of the world. The Max 737 requires high-performance parts produced by elite manufacturers, which were dependent on those contracts and hit hard by the Boeing shutdown. When production began again, Boeing was uncertain if those producers were going to be able to deliver, not only because of the interruption in their business with Boeing but due to their countries' struggles with COVID-19. It was a large rift in the supply chain that didn't exist before.

Takeaways

- Marco Polo and his routes along the Silk Road in the thirteenth century provided evidence of the value of international trade and set the world on course toward a global economy.
- Nations do better by trading with other nations because trading partners can capitalize on their strengths while addressing their weaknesses.
- Despite the growth of emerging nations with huge populations, like China and India, the United States remains relatively rich as a world technology leader.

Equilibrium

We live in a world that has been interconnected for a long time. Different parts of the world are good at doing different things, and those differences made trade advantageous—I can trade what I'm good at with you for what you're good at. Standards of living rise with the resulting trade relationships. Innovations, both physical and intellectual, have always eventually spread around the world, but it seems to be happening faster now.

The United States has had a long history of being good at applying new innovations in its economy and it has resulted in a high standard of living that is shared by a relatively small percentage of the world's population. But that disparity is not static, and has not been static for longer than the history of the United States. What happens over there matters over here and vice-versa.

CHAPTER 3

Politics and the Economy

Intellectuals have been pontificating about the economy forever, the first known reference to supply and demand being in the fourth century BC in Aristophanes' comedy, *Frogs*. But the beginnings of our modern concept of economics can be attributed to Adam Smith, a Scottish professor of moral philosophy at the University of Glasgow, lecturing on the "political economy" in the late eighteenth century.

Smith's renown is in identifying what constitutes wealth for a nation. The prevailing view of his era, mercantilism, was that wealth equaled gold; a country became wealthy by exporting more than it imported, and by doing so, accumulating gold. Instead, Smith professed, a nation's wealth comes from its productive capacity. As opposed to piles of gold, a nation should accumulate capabilities it can employ to make and sell exponentially more goods and services.

The Pin Factory

Smith famously opened his *An Inquiry into the Nature and Causes of the Wealth of Nations*, his treatise on the political economy published in 1776, with a description of the workings of a "pin factory":

> One man draws out the wire, another straights it, a third cuts it, a fourth points it, a fifth grinds it at the top for receiving the head; to make the head requires two or three distinct operations; to put it on, is a peculiar business, to whiten the pins is another; it is even a trade by itself to put them into the paper; and the important business of making a pin is, in this manner, divided into about eighteen distinct operations, which, in some manufactories, are all performed by distinct hands.

One person making pins has to cut the wire, sharpen the wire, put on the head—do all the processes. But a capitalist will invest in a number of employees who do one part of the process each. By separating the duties and assigning each to a specialist, the gains in productivity are enormous. Of course, you have to have a market for your pins; you have to aggressively trade to reach all those people who want pins. The ability to combine production and specialization with trade—that is, to manufacture and sell—is the key to growing wealth, Smith proposed. You can supply the world with your pins, and all the trading partners benefit.

Free Trade and Limited Government

The Wealth of Nations' premise that free trade is the basis for national prosperity caught the attention of the elite intellectual classes in Europe and America. To Smith, the principle of free trade included limiting the role of government in the economy, an idea already gaining steam among Europeans tiring of their monarchs controlling the nation's purse strings. Smith would replace what the monarchs wanted with what the markets demanded. Government was better suited for enabling free markets: mounting a national defense, building roads and other infrastructure, establishing a court system, and making and enforcing laws, which, in terms of the economy, meant dealing with fraud and abuse.

In essence, the role of government would be limited to only those things that a free enterprise system could not readily establish on its own. That implied that trade should be free of government intervention, including tariffs that distort what the market is trying to achieve, that redirect trade. Smith didn't like the idea of increasing prices just because a product crosses a political border. The market would control pricing, as if by an invisible hand, attracting entrepreneurs when prices are high, resulting in increased production and lower prices.

Smith was not blind to the perils of unfettered capitalism. He warned in *The Wealth of Nations* that, "There is seldom a case where business people meet that doesn't end in a conspiracy to raise prices on the general public." He was aware that business needs a watchdog, but, given the government's role in enforcing a level playing field, the market would provide guidance, overseeing and filtering production to the benefit of all.

Political Tug of War

The term "political economy" aptly describes the tug of war between public health issues and what was required to address impending economic concerns accompanying the COVID-19 pandemic of 2020. In the short and long runs, the objectives of both health and economic policy makers were identical; you can't have a thriving economy if everyone is sick. But the effort to find the right balance was political in nature. New Zealand, for example, took an aggressive stance in containing the spread of the virus and initially took a hard economic hit, then opened up faster than other industrial economies that were less aggressive in combating the pandemic initially and had more prolonged economic distress.

Closing down commerce for improvements in people's health comes at a cost. But how much of the economy needs to be shut down in the short term to promote long-term health? As the pandemic roared through the United States and around the world, there was no clear answer to that question.

Takeaways

- Adam Smith changed the way Western society thought about the economy, from accommodating the potential whims of a monarch to letting a free market exercise its muscle.
- The shift implied limiting government's role in determining a nation's economic activity, including distorting prices by imposing tariffs on market-driven free trade, and allowing free markets to make production and allocation decisions.

Equilibrium

The leading economies of the world have not always been capitalistic or free-market oriented, and defining a "leading economy" has always been a popular subject of debate. For centuries, economies were under the control of the ruler or monarch whose decisions, particularly about international trade and domestic production, had great influence on the well-being of the populace. The discipline of economics was spurred in the eighteenth century by Adam Smith's *The Wealth of Nations*, which argued that free markets typically made better decisions about production and trade than monarchs, and that the wealth of nations was not about the stock of gold in the royal vaults, but rather was about the productive capacity of the domestic economy. Smith and his early followers maintained that people's differing preferences and abilities would sort themselves out into a grand equilibrium that could produce a better result than even the most insightful and benevolent set of rules established by the government.

PART II
GDP and Consumption

CHAPTER 4

GDP: The Perfectly Imperfect Measurement

Gross domestic product (GDP) is likely the most featured, argued over, concerning, and sometimes even misleading economic indicator. A measure of the value of all final goods and services produced in an economy, GDP is as important as it is imperfect. The annual growth in GDP, expressed as a percentage, is our proxy for how the economy is doing. But it is not a definitive metric for economic well-being; it is compromised by a number of shortcomings.

There are two ways to measure GDP: real and nominal. Real GDP is the figure we hear most, that number bandied about quarterly or at the end of a year as the measure of the country's economic progress. "Real" is considered the better measurement of underlying activity because it gauges the actual change in the quantity of goods and services produced—that is, it adjusts for inflation—while nominal GDP is the tally of spending on final goods and services and thus can be enlarged by inflation.

Nominal GDP is less preferred because spending changes for two reasons: you're either buying more things or paying more because of inflation. If nominal GDP increases by 2 percent and inflation over the same period is also 2 percent, real GDP is zero. There is no real growth. Both measures are important to monitor, but changes in real GDP tell us how much more (or less) is being produced.

By focusing on the final sales of goods and services GDP keeps us from being misled by double counting. For example, buying a car. The automobile you buy comes with tires; they're an "intermediate good." They are produced, of course, but if you count them as goods sold on their own, then count the purchase price of the car at its sale, you're double-counting the tires—not to mention the many other parts that get made, sold to the auto manufacturer, and built into your car.

The Good and Bad in GDP

GDP is most valuable as a consistent scorecard over time, measuring the difference in production from one period to the next, or more importantly, to the previous period. Again, it might not be perfect, but it is consistent, and having a consistent and agreed upon measure for economic output is a vital part of understanding economies and making economic policy. Being able to judge relative economic performance across time and nations is vital to improving macroeconomic performance.

That said, GDP has its defects. For one, the number typically reported doesn't measure growth per capita. Economic output is a function of the number of workers producing goods and services and the amount of capital and technology they have to work with. Consider farming in the United States, now compared to a century ago. The United States produces more food today than ever, but it does it in a much more capital-intensive way. In 1900 there were thousands of small farms and thousands more farm workers. In the twenty-first century, there is a much greater concentration of output in fewer, larger farms with much more invested in capital and technology than workers. Our current standard of living reflects that increase in per capita output. We care about the pie getting larger, but we care more about the per capita slice getting bigger.

A good example of the difference between real and nominal GDP comes from our neighbor to the south. Mexico saw rather rapid real GDP growth in the 1970s, with several years of more than 7 percent real growth. In subsequent years, growth results were mixed, with several negative periods, two of which saw the economy contract by more than 5 percent (See Figure 4.1).

In comparing real GDP to Mexican real GDP per capita for the same period, the fundamental picture looks similar—the economy is much more volatile than the population—but there are notable differences. In the 1970s, per capita growth, while strong, was only above 7 percent one year, much of the strength in that decade muted by rapid population growth. At the same time, the downturns were worse: four declines at or worse than 5 percent, the two most severe at 7 percent or worse (See Figure 4.2).

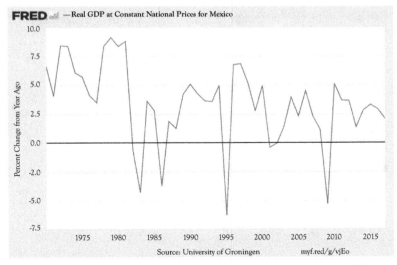

Figure 4.1 Annual rates of Mexican real GDP growth from 1970

Source: University of California, Davis

Release: Penn World Table 9.1

Units: Millions of 2011 U.S. Dollars, Not Seasonally Adjusted

Frequency: Annual

Source: Feenstra, R.C., I. Robert, and M.P. Timmer. 2015. "The Next Generation of the Penn World Table." *American Economic Review* 105, no. 10, 3150–3182, available for download at www. ggdc.net/pwtFor more information, see http://rug.nl/research/ggdc/data/pwt/

University of Groningen and University of California, Davis,

Real GDP at Constant National Prices for Mexico [RGDPNAMXA666NRUG],

Retrieved from FRED,

Federal Reserve Bank of St. Louis;

https://fred.stlouisfed.org/series/RGDPNAMXA666NRUG,

September 15, 2020.

Another drawback to measuring the economy via GDP is the enormous amount of production that doesn't get counted. Part of the increase in GDP in the United States has resulted from a shift toward monetizing production that used to be done at home. If you clean your own house, it doesn't get counted in GDP, but it does if you hire a maid service. The output is the same in both cases, but we see an increase in GDP as more and more people outsource work they used to do themselves. In developing economies, a large amount of output doesn't get counted because it is done within the family unit.

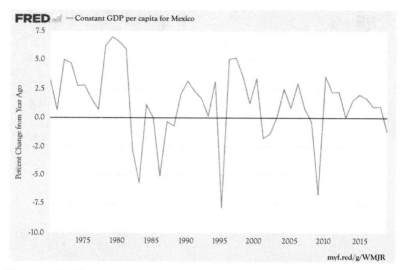

Figure 4.2 Mexican Real GDP per capita from 1970 to 2020 (pre-COVID)

Source: World Bank.

Release: World Development Indicators

Units: 2010 U.S. Dollars, Not Seasonally Adjusted

Frequency: Annual

GDP per capita is gross domestic product divided by midyear population. GDP is the sum of gross value-added by all resident producers in the economy plus any product taxes and minus any subsidies not included in the value of the products. It is calculated without making deductions for depreciation of fabricated assets or for depletion and degradation of natural resources. World Bank national accounts data, and OECD National Accounts data files.

World Bank,

Constant GDP per capita for Mexico [NYGDPPCAPKDMEX],

Retrieved from FRED,

Federal Reserve Bank of St. Louis;

https://fred.stlouisfed.org/series/NYGDPPCAPKDMEX,

September 15, 2020.

As well, GDP doesn't include "negative externalities," things that subtract from our standard of living. The value of steel produced in a steel mill gets counted in GDP, but the consequences of the mill's dirty smokestack don't. The pollution occurs because of activity that is boosting GDP, but the problems and costs associated with the pollution are rarely included in calculating GDP. Traffic congestion imposes time costs on commuters and health costs due to stress and pollution. But as congestion

increases, GDP increases with more gasoline sales, increased car mainte-
nance expenditures, and consumption of other goods like take-out foods
that will ease the waiting. Consider the decades of negative externalities
produced by the makers of cigarettes. The U.S. tobacco industry was large
and dominant worldwide. It made large contributions to GDP. But the
negative externality of smoking, the resulting diseases, wasn't included
as an offset. In fact, the spending on healthcare to deal with some of the
consequences of smoking served to boost GDP.

Cigarettes are the tip of another GDP iceberg. It doesn't consider an
economy's citizens' well-being. Health issues are problematic in measurement, and various attempts to measure happiness and other aspects of
well-being don't always correlate with relative GDP. To be fair, wealthier
countries tend to do better in health metrics, but the correlation isn't perfect and in recent years health metrics have been declining in the United
States even as the economy was quite robust.

Nor does GDP address income distribution. Of enormous recent
concern in the United States and other advanced economies is the unequal
distribution of economic gains. While some inequality is inevitable—people
may choose to do things, like attend college or not attend college; or have
to do things, like stay home to care for an ailing parent, that contribute to
inequality—the distribution of income over the last few decades has not
added to the incomes of large segments of the U.S. workforce. GDP, by
itself, is incapable of capturing that inequality.

Then we have the much-ballyhooed underground economy. By definition it is difficult to count, and therefore not usually recognized in
GDP, at least not directly—that is, you don't have audited verification.
You can find estimates of the amount of unreported production, but they
are unreliable.

Bigger Pie, Bigger Slices

Despite the large number of shortcomings in the measure, a larger GDP
can be instrumental in remedying many of those problems. Increasing
the cost of the production of certain goods in order to address pollution is a much easier task in a wealthy economy where those added
costs are proportionately smaller and less impactful than in some poorer

economies. Income distribution issues are easier to address when incomes overall are increasing.

It's easy to criticize GDP as a true and accurate measurement of a nation's economy. But its defects are well understood; economists know it as an imperfect measurement. But it is also understood that GDP growth is necessary, if not sufficient on its own, to make a country and its citizens better off. If it is falling, or if it doesn't keep pace with population growth, someone has to give something up, which is problematic for the rich and even more so for the poor. If the pie is getting bigger, you might get a bigger slice without others having to settle for less.

Looking Ahead

Broadly defined, GDP is divided into four categories: consumption, investment, government, and net exports. All final goods and services are accounted for by one of those categories: cars and carrots, consumption; a house, investment; roads and public schools, government. And if we're selling more to our trading partners than them to us, the difference is a net gain in GDP—or a net loss if we have a trade deficit. Those four categories are where all the action is, and each deserves a deep dive, which is where we are headed in Chapters 5 through 19.

Takeaways

- GDP is not a perfect measurement of how an economy is growing or contracting.
- But real GDP is generally considered a good measure of how a nation's economy is doing, providing a consistent scorecard over time, measuring the difference in production from one quarter or year to the same period the previous year.
- Among its defects, GDP does not measure growth per capita, income distribution, negative externalities or the underground economy.
- But GDP growth is necessary to improve the lot of a nation and its citizens.

Equilibrium

GDP is how we have agreed to keep score on the output of an economy. It is a far from perfect measure, but it is rather consistent both over time and across countries, which makes it useful for evaluating the performance of an economy over time and performance across economies. A simple naive application of the metric is useful in a large number of circumstances, and having a deeper understanding of the measure's virtues and defects allows for nuance in interpreting results. Just as a speedometer does not tell you everything about the performance of your car, it does provide vital information that is helpful in evaluating your journey.

CHAPTER 5

Consumers and Consumption: Follow the Money

Great Britain's John Maynard Keynes was one of the most influential economists of all time—his most influential work, *The General Theory of Employment, Interest and Money*, published in 1935. A macroeconomist, he developed theories shaped by the major global events of the time, in particular the Great Depression, the rumblings leading up to World War II, then the war itself and the postwar period of exponential global productivity growth. In a 1930 essay titled, *The Economic Possibilities for our Grandchildren*, Keynes, reflecting on the nature of the twentieth century's macroeconomic productivity surge, predicted that by the twenty-first century the average developed country workweek would be fifteen hours. We simply wouldn't need more than that to satisfy our needs.

Indeed, pro-labor movements post–World War II won a forty-hour workweek. But efforts to cutback hours even further fizzled, even though the "free world" continued to make huge strides in productivity on a per capita basis—the surge slowed some in the 1970s and 1980s—more than enough to fulfill Keynes' vision. Yet we persisted with our eight-hours-a-day, five-days-a-week schedules. As opposed to less work, we demanded more goods and services.

More Work, More Income, More Products and Services

Advances in production and technology changed what we now think of as "basic" needs. Keynes couldn't have foreseen that by the turn of the next century it would be nearly impossible to function in business and society without a smart phone. Our consumption standards far exceed what Keynes and his contemporaries thought they would be. Which is why we work, so we can make more goods and services and buy more goods and services. Many of our consumption decisions might not be in our best interests, but they are ours, and many people would like to consume more—many need more—if they could only have more income to spend.

What we do with what we earn is a matter of discussion that extends beyond economics to how marketing creates demand and new opportunities. Some complain that marketing has created a passion for unnecessary, even unhealthy products, like sugary drinks and fatty foods. But there are products like portable computers and mobile phones that had to be marketed because they were unfamiliar technology when introduced and that turned out to be remarkably useful. The Apple Watch, once the stuff of science fiction—think Dick Tracy and his 2-Way Wrist TV-Radio—is available and with many practical features, but people had to be marketed to in order to learn about it.

More than a century ago, U.S. economist Thorstein Veblen coined the term "conspicuous consumption." In his *The Theory of the Leisure Class*, published in 1899, he proposed that a great deal of consumption by the wealthy is a way to display conspicuously that they are well off. By doing so they achieve some social advantage. Wildly expensive watches—Rolexes come to most minds—serve as a good example. They differ from an Apple Watch that also has an element of social cache, including its sports band, but is more useful in that it tracks how far you walk, lets you pay a bill, even replaces your car key. The Rolex might tell you the time if you remember to set it, while the Apple Watch adjusts its time automatically not only to when but where you are.

Consumption is also governed by availability, an issue that particularly affects consumers in low-income countries and low-income U.S. neighborhoods. Availability determines to a great degree the kind of food we eat, which in turn influences our need for healthcare products and services; if there's nothing other than junk food available in your neighborhood, the cost of traveling to another neighborhood for healthier food can be prohibitively high. Broadening access to products and services is another reason for people to work more in order to earn more.

Consumption in Emerging Markets

Personal consumption of goods and services accounts for about 70 percent of U.S. GDP. In a relatively wealthy, capital-rich economy, personal consumption items can account for a high share of overall spending. But in an emerging market, more of the income is spent on adding to the capital stock and improving infrastructure. Spending is dedicated to enhancing productivity, which should ultimately give each worker an opportunity to earn more. We have an abundance of capital in the United States, enough to be comfortable that we will have access to drinkable water and drivable roads (although, sadly, we fall short of meeting such fundamental needs in some locations). We don't need to devote as large a share of our economy to investment in capital or public goods as emerging economies.

The most advanced economies are also on the leading edge of technology investment. That's what it means to be advanced. But there are plusses and minuses to taking the lead. Sometimes advances become obsolete before other slower economies even start to invest in the technology. The United States invested heavily in wire to bring telephone service and cable TV networks into homes across the country. Wire enabled a significant advance that delivered substantial benefits. But it has largely outlived its usefulness as a transmitter of audio, video, and digital signals. Emerging nations that had not invested in copper wire networks are going directly to wireless communication. The relative investment pay-off can change dramatically and the relative share of consumption versus what you're investing in can change across time and space. Taking the lead sometimes means bearing costs followers can avoid.

Takeaways

- People work to be able to consume.
- In rich nations personal consumption represents the bulk of what is made, bought and sold.
- In the United States, consumers are responsible for 70 percent of the nation's GDP, so monitoring U.S. consumption is key to understanding where the economy is in terms of growth.

Equilibrium

Consumption is fundamentally why we work. We need income to buy food, shelter, virtually everything vital to our existence. We purchase other things as well, some more essential than others, some of which may not be for ourselves. We spend in altruistic ways for the betterment of society. We spend on things that aren't good for us over time. We may also save some of our income to enjoy consumption at some later time.

Our income, at least for some segments of industrialized economies, has grown substantially over the last few centuries, though that income increase is often subject to deficiencies in how it is distributed. Our ability to find outlets for our additional income has grown too and kept pace with income growth.

CHAPTER 6

Shifting Sands: Consumers Prefer Services

Now that we've toured the realm of GDP, let's take note of the elephant in the castle. Americans are champion spenders. Overall, personal consumption totals about 70 percent of our domestic economy.

According to a March 2019 *GOBankingRates* study, Americans spend an average $103 a day per person. Much of that goes to housing payments—then there's getting the kids ready for school and driving to work and making dinner. But we also spend a startling sum on beer and pizza.

Gallup's final study of consumer spending—the pollster stopped tracking U.S. consumer spending in July 2017—revealed how we dispose of a considerable amount of our disposable income:

- $41.8 billion on fishing trips, $81 billion on bicycle trips, and $12 billion on rock climbing and hiking trips—then $76.3 billion treating trips and falls
- $13.5 billion on cosmetic surgery and—you might not think we'd need so much of it after all that—$62 billion on cosmetics
- $2.7 billion at food trucks, then $2 billion treating acid indigestion (okay, not necessarily connected)
- $223.5 billion on alcohol and alcohol-related costs (accidents, drunk driving fines, trips to the emergency room, and so on)

Yes, we're at a high end of the consuming range for modern-day industrial economies—United Kingdom residents averaged $65 a day; Chinese citizens were consuming at a rate of less than $16 daily. But those inequities are seldom trumpeted and haven't sounded many alarms. In a functional sense, we work to be able to consume, and in the relatively advanced, wealthy economy we enjoy, it is reasonable to expect a higher share of output to be devoted to our own wants and needs over physical capital and infrastructure.

The state of the labor market plays a crucial role in determining spending behavior. When people consume, they make their decisions based on their expectations for future income: confident, spend away; not so confident, cut back. A tight labor market breeds confidence. If you're in a job you might not have for long, or might not want for long, and you look around to find plentiful opportunities, you're more likely to spend and possibly take on debt.

One of the more interesting aspects of the recovery from the Great Recession of 2008 and 2009 was our caution. Consumer spending did not surge the way it had in previous U.S. recoveries. It has been the case that recoveries in the United States have been proportional to the recessions themselves—that is, the steeper the recession the more aggressive the recovery. It's that "pent-up demand." During a recession consumption gets postponed or delayed because of concerns about personal income, and when the recession is over and people are confident again about their future employment and income, they make up for lost consuming. This didn't happen in the recovery from the Great Recession. Consumers were wary of taking on debt after working it down during the recession and increased their spending only about as much as their incomes increased. This lack of a spending burst at the end of the recession earned the recovery its characterization, and criticism, as a "slow" recovery.

If consumers disappointed critics by their post-recession hesitancy, consumer balance sheets in 2019, in aggregate, were in relatively good shape. Americans were financially healthy. Of course, there were caveats. Many Americans were dealing with considerable debt. But aggregate personal debt was relatively low compared to income, and in combination with historically low interest rates, provided for historically low debt service to income ratios—that is, payments due on outstanding debt compared to income—as explained in Figure 6.1.

What We Buy and Why

You can divide what consumers buy into three classes: nondurable goods, durable goods, and services.

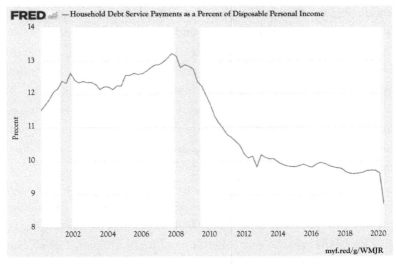

Figure 6.1 *Low aggregate personal debt combined with low interest rates to reduce debt service to income ratios to historic lows by 2020*

Source: Board of Governors of the Federal Reserve System (US)

Release: Household Debt Service and Financial Obligations Ratios

Units: Percent, Seasonally Adjusted

Frequency: Quarterly

For further information please visit the Board of Governors.

Board of Governors of the Federal Reserve System (US),

Household Debt Service Payments as a Percent of Disposable Personal Income [TDSP],

Retrieved from FRED,

Federal Reserve Bank of St. Louis;

https://fred.stlouisfed.org/series/TDSP,

November 19, 2020.

Nondurable goods are things like food, energy, and clothing (despite seeing Uncle Walter in the same sweater every Christmas for the last ten years). These items are basic to human existence, but they also represent a decreasing share of our overall consumption bundle. When our income goes up, we move on to other things: dining out, vacations, a nicer house, or just a new washing machine.

Tracking nondurable goods consumption isn't particularly interesting from a macroeconomic perspective. There's a fair amount of variation in spending on things like energy, where prices are volatile; but as an advanced economy, most of us consume all the nondurable goods we want. Our problem isn't that we're starving but that we have enough money to make bad food choices. The most meaningful feature of nondurable goods consumption is the seasonal variation in our patterns of consumption, particularly at year-end, around the holidays.

Durable goods are things that last. Think major appliances or autos. Here too, their share of our larger consumption bundle is declining. Still, sales of durable goods are important to watch for two reasons.

First, they tend to be expensive, and consequently have a bigger impact on GDP. When you buy a durable good, the entire purchase price shows up in the national income accounts even though the useful life of that good stretches over a long period of time.

Durable goods can create shadowy volatility in the quarterly GDP numbers simply due to timing. For example, when the cash-for-clunkers program was initiated under the Obama administration to get aging gas guzzlers off the road and encourage the consumption of more fuel-efficient new cars, we saw a considerable spike in auto sales, which consequently led to a transitory increase, that is, a temporary spike, in GDP. When you take delivery of a new car it has thousands of dollars of impact on GDP. If it happens on the last day of the third quarter, GDP jumps that amount for that period, if it happens on the first day of the fourth quarter, GDP jumps for that quarter. If it happens on a large enough scale, it reveals why we see volatility in quarterly GDP reports and why those reports can be misleading in the short run. Volatility tends to smooth itself out over a long enough period of time.

The second reason we keep a close watch on durable goods sales is because the products are expensive and long-lived. The decision to buy a new durable good or fix an old one tells us something about another popular—if of limited value because it is dominated by recent, short-term developments—economic measuring stick, consumer confidence. If consumers are feeling good about the economy, they'll commit and upgrade their existing durable goods; if they're concerned about their future income streams, they'll repair rather than replace.

Services: The Biggest Share and Growing

The largest share of our consumption spending is for services. The spending share of services grew from 46 percent in 1959 to 67 percent in 2019, while the share of nondurable goods dropped from 40 percent to

25 percent. As our income rises, we tend to want others to do things for us that we can't or don't want to do. When we get a raise we'll use some of that money to enjoy a dinner out instead of buying more carrots. We have all the carrots we want, so an increase in our income isn't going to change our carrot consumption (unless we're talking diamonds).

The demand for some services can be explained by natural forces like demographics. The U.S. population is aging; the aging population needs medical care. It's necessary that we consume more medical services—and with rising income levels, we can shift our consumption bundle in that direction. It's not that we're decreasing our consumption of durable and nondurable goods, but the additional consumption is in services. And again, in aggregate—not all Americans are so fortunate—we are wealthy enough to afford it.

Measuring real economic output in the service sector is problematic. It's easy to track the nominal spending on services, but that nominal spending reflects a combination of spending on an actual service and the change in its price. Disentangling price movement from a real change in output is the challenge.

Again, medical services illustrate the point. They're going up in price but they're also going up in quality. How do we distinguish between the two? Serious trauma accidents are health events that were once fatal but now, frequently, treatable. The price of treatment has increased, but we're getting improved outcomes. You're spending more but you're buying a better product. Clearly, the real output of healthcare services is increasing, but by how much?

The question applies to many services. Most of us enjoy a wider and better choice of restaurants where we live. But how much of our spending on food outside the household represents an increase in the quality of the food and restaurant experience, and how much is simply our willingness to pay a nominally higher price because we don't want to cook?

One of the most difficult services to measure for changes in output is security. We spend a lot on security, but it doesn't produce any real output. If it works, nothing happens. What's the value of that nothing? Immense. Consider the growing need and skyrocketing costs for cyber-security. If customers of a local construction business have their financial data stolen from that company's computers, it could, and frequently has, put the company out of business. But implementing a cybersecurity program is costly, and if no data thief attacks, what's it worth? So, we continue to increase our spending on security, but measuring the value of that output is extremely difficult.

More and more frequently, services involve paying people to do something we otherwise would have done ourselves. If you're a do-it-yourselfer, you don't pay yourself, and consequently the output associated with your effort isn't captured in GDP. But it does show up when you pay a service provider to do it.

Takeaways

- Personal consumption spending, if for no other reason than volume, deserves a disproportionate share of attention when trying to understand economic growth in the U.S. economy.
- Consumption as a relatively high share of GDP is an advantage of living in an advanced economy, even if it does comes with risks that require attention.

Equilibrium

Our tastes and preferences for the things we spend our money on can change over time based on new innovations in products and services, and based on what we have already consumed. A large segment of consumers are secure in their food, clothing, shelter, and electronic gizmos, and we are seeing an increasing share of consumption devoted to services, to employing other people to do things for us. But not all the shift toward services is about already having enough goods. An aging population requires more services. This is particularly evident in health care, where the shift to more service-intense consumption is reflected in our need for more medical services.

CHAPTER 7

Great Expectations

You're up in the morning and getting ready for the day ahead. The forecast is for a chillier temperature than yesterday and afternoon rain, so you dress in warm clothes, throw an umbrella in the car, and cancel your three o'clock tee time. Those expectations might not be realized, but they affect your preparation and plans for the day.

The same applies to the macroeconomy. In Chapter 6, we addressed the importance of personal consumption to the U.S. economy. Much of what people spend is determined by what they expect their future incomes to be. If they are confident their incomes will increase, they are likely to behave consistent with that expectation. Someone anticipating a promotion and raise might buy a car or move into a bigger house, or take the family on a more luxurious vacation and eat out at restaurants more often.

But what impacts the economy more than great expectations is what happens when the outlook is not so hopeful. If you fear you might lose your job, or an illness or injury threatens your future earnings, you'll stop spending and start saving. When that happens on a national scale, when the markets are heading south or TV prognosticators are predicting an economic downturn, the mere expectation can be self-fulfilling. When enough people become convinced that a recession is on the horizon and stop spending, GDP contracts and we get that recession. It might not be caused by some fundamental weakness in the economy or negative event, only by how consumers behave. Self-fulfilling expectations, both positive and negative, have a major influence on the course of the economy.

Expectations and Business

Expectations play a central role in business decisions. Any serious investment decision in based on an organization's expectations of future profitability. Even a decision as seemingly trivial as a store's operating hours is based in large part on expectations of when customers will arrive.

What markets are going to be interested in funding, what investors will be interested in investing in, consumer trends: all are based on expectations. Well-founded or not, they shape business decisions. Many don't turn out as expected. Founders and investors spend millions making products that don't win consumers' hearts. Think *Edsel*. And all those companies that combined to burst the dot-com bubble in the late 1990s because they couldn't find their way from startups to making money. The investments that brought those products to market were based on expectations that, in the end, turned out to be wrong.

Great companies have registered colossal failures. The instant success of Apple's *Macintosh*—sales reached 70,000 units barely three months after its release—followed on the heels of a colossal failure. *Lisa*, named after Apple Founder Steve Jobs' daughter and developed at an estimated cost of more than 50 million 1970s dollars, was abandoned shortly after its release in 1983. There are many more who have faded into anonymity, generating considerable GDP in their making but no lasting wealth.

Apple is the standard bearer for companies that persist despite mixed expectations. There was a great deal of skepticism surrounding Apple computers, then the iPhone, but Jobs believed that once people understood what Apple's products did for them, sales would soar. So he invested heavily to make the products, then market the products, and the rest, as they say, is history—and history in the making.

Investors and Markets

Investors are betting on what will happen in the future. How a stock is expected to perform in the months and years ahead is reflected in the current stock price.

Expectation explains, to some extent, what befuddled so many Americans in the summer of 2020 as the equity markets rose while the COVID-19 pandemic spread, unemployment climbed to record levels, and economists predicted a U.S. recession. The market plunged in March—three days of the worst point drops in U.S. history. The expected recession was being priced into the market. Then, when employment reports started to turn, a brighter outlook moved stock prices higher.

It was the outlook for a quicker or faster future recovery and not the presently unfolding recession that moved stocks.

Expectation also explains, at least partially, why stock markets were so volatile in 2020—and likely to remain so as the Fed promised to keep its benchmark interest rate at or near zero for an extended period of time. When interest rates are low, changes in future values have more impact on a stock's present value calculation. Changes in expected future earnings are magnified in terms of the present value because future gains will be less eroded by current lower interest rates. Again, the combination of low interest rates and future expectations is not a complete explanation of volatility; there are other factors, including inflation and the Fisher effect, which we'll address in Chapter 32. Overall, however, you can rely on financial markets to be much more volatile than the economy.

Expectations and Reality

In the early stages of the spread of COVID-19 throughout the United States, there was a run on toilet paper. To put it delicately, overall demand did not increase. The virus, in fact, was a respiratory disease, so we might have anticipated a run on facial tissues. The shortage was created purely by expectation. Distribution was the issue, but while producers scrambled to shift tissue packaged for office use to packaging tissue for retail sales, consumers who didn't rush to hoard supplies had to find alternative means to obtain toilet paper. (One of the authors' wives shipped rolls via UPS from Atlanta to friends in Orlando.) The expectation of a potential shortage was sufficient to produce a shortage in reality, even though the fundamental production and consumption of the underlying product was essentially unchanged.

Takeaways

- Expectations, founded or not, fulfilled or not, drive much of the macroeconomy. What we expect to happen to our incomes in the future will to a great extent determine how we spend today.

- Expectations drive business decisions. Producers will produce and investors invest in products or services that promise to garner broad acceptance in their marketplaces.
- Unfulfilled expectations can result in negative externalities to a nation's GDP, while some expectations that prove unfounded and even irrational generate substantial demand and increase GDP.

Equilibrium

Expectations, both when they are right and when they are wrong, drive a huge share of our decisions. We buy goods and services with certain expectations about what we will receive, and whether or not the expectation is met is crucial to further transactions. Expectations that turn out to be incorrect will motivate a different behavior in the future, while if they are fulfilled, we may see a repeat of the behavior. Thus, how we form our expectations and to what extent they are correct are essential to equilibrium in the economy. If expectations are widely disappointed, the equilibrium outcome for the economy will be far different than if expectations were met.

CHAPTER 8

Saving and Investing: Equilibrium at Work

During of the second quarter of 2020, the personal savings rate in the United States jumped to 25.6 percent; the annual average for 2019 was 7.9 percent. So people saved slightly more than a quarter of their disposable personal income in Q2 2020 compared to about one-thirteenth the previous year. Consumers responded to COVID-19 by increasing their savings and reducing their spending. Some of it was unintentional, as some types of spending were virtually eliminated, like travel and dining out. But people also cut back intentionally out of concern over layoffs and furloughs and getting through uncertain times. Those savings then made their way into some form of investment.

Investment takes many forms. There are investments in tangible items, like plant equipment or government and nongovernment infrastructure projects, or inventories. Or intangibles, such as research and development and the resulting intellectual property, or human capital, including time and money spent on education and training. Regardless of the form it takes, most investing is intended to make the economy more productive, to make us better off than we would be without it—even if it doesn't always work out that way.

Investment is made possible by savings, which, by definition, means abstaining from consuming some of your, or a business's, after-tax income. We know that we need to save to invest, and we want to be rewarded for investing to the benefit of the economy. But since the financial crisis in 2008, interest rates have been at or near zero, and the reward for saving has been small. An entire generation has gone unrewarded for abstaining from consumption, which is likely to have long-term implications for savings and investment in the United States and around the world.

But there are still strong motives for setting something aside. Simple precautionary balances—a rainy day fund—are a prudent part of planning for life, as is the prospect of retirement and being able to sustain a lifestyle similar to how you live before you stop earning.

When you save, the money you put aside is financial capital. You take money from your earnings and deposit it in some financial intermediary, like a bank. In turn the bank lends it to someone or some organization that is part of the larger system of financial markets, thereby matching up your savings with borrowers. The markets transform those monetary savings into "real investment" that firms convert into tangible and intangible products and services, or pass along to others interested in investing in some form of capital or needing to borrow money for some period of time.

What Do People, Governments, and Businesses Invest In?

Governments invest in tangible assets like infrastructure and intangible assets like educating their populations. Individuals might invest in their own education or form public–private partnerships to invest in infrastructure. They might also directly invest in business by buying stocks or bonds, or indirectly invest by giving their savings to a financial intermediary like a bank or a mutual fund to manage for them. Businesses invest in tangible assets like offices and machines to become more productive, and in intangible assets like technology, employees, and training.

The decision to invest must consider two dimensions: what to invest in and when to invest in it. For example, a manufacturing firm's state-of-the-art technology could be rendered obsolete by a new invention, so it might want to hold off investing in the new technology until its capacity to improve productivity and its role in its industry are clarified. Or the manufacturer might want to invest in existing technology to better serve its current market.

Many emerging nations don't invest in cutting-edge technology because it is expensive and they are growing rapidly with a less current and less expensive technology. They are willing to wait until their economies require the cutting-edge technology to remain competitive and continue growing. Coordinating those decisions over time is difficult yet necessary for long-term growth and productivity.

Socially Responsible Investing

In principle, people want the highest possible return on their savings, adjusted for risk and other factors. But the "highest return" has many dimensions, not only dollars. Investors invest in order to maximize what economists call expected utility, essentially a multi-dimensional measure of happiness or well-being. Surely, more money is a big part of that, but there are other rewards that are just as or more important to investors than nominal returns. It's why dollar returns on tobacco, firearms and oil have to be higher to attract investors, because they are often viewed as repugnant industries. On the other hand, green energy companies have attracted investors despite a lower financial yield because people are willing to take less money in exchange for the satisfaction they get for doing what they feel is the right thing. People don't want to buy cars that pollute, and Elon Musk and Tesla have had no problem attracting investors and buyers.

Economist Milton Friedman, who won the Nobel Prize for Economics in 1976, has been roundly criticized for proposing that companies should be concerned about nothing but shareholder value, that they aren't in business to effect social change. But as prone as he was to such unfiltered pronouncements, there's more subtlety in his argument than meets the ear. He often argued that socially superior goods offer superior returns because they do better in the market, and that the market ultimately will not reward a producer for making something socially repugnant.

Investing in goods and services you believe in won't be rewarding if the market disagrees with your preferences. You might hold squid in high regard, but if your taste isn't shared, you probably shouldn't invest in Squid Lovers International, Inc.

More than Meets the Eye

Investment returns are also affected by things the company you are investing in has little control over. Agricultural businesses face multiple inherent global risks. ConAgra has a major stake in grain production in the

United States but is also affected by the volume of grain being produced in Brazil. Global weather patterns are also a major agribusiness risk factor. Solar panel production seems like a growth industry, and therefore a good investment. But manufacturers in the United States face formidable competition from abroad, particularly from China where extreme pollution has heightened the need for and substantially advanced clean energy production. Investors weigh all these issues—financial, moral, and ethical—to determine a risk-adjusted rate of return.

While money is fungible and can flow easily across borders, it often doesn't. Savings can remain in a particular economy at unduly high levels, a phenomenon known as "home country bias." Investors physically located in economies tend to keep savings produced there at home as opposed to financing activities in other countries, even though those investments may offer higher risk-adjusted returns. Home country bias is not always the most effective practice, but it happens, even when an investor can generate a higher rate of return elsewhere.

In the next three chapters we will examine in greater depth the key beneficiaries of modern investment, real estate, intellectual capital, and inventory, and how the principle of equilibrium works in intended and unintended ways.

Takeaways

- Investments take many forms and are made possible by savings, the portion of your after-tax income you don't dedicate to consumption.
- Investors must consider two dimensions in their decision-making: what to invest and when to invest.
- People want the highest possible return on their savings, but "highest return" has many dimensions and should be thought of as "expected utility," a measure of happiness or well-being. People may be willing to take less money in exchange for the satisfaction they get for doing what they feel is the right thing.
- Some investors practice "home country bias" investing, keeping their money invested in their home country, even though they can get higher risk-adjusted financial returns investing elsewhere.

Equilibrium

Savings and investment is where the concept of equilibrium gains real traction. People receive income for producing GDP and, if they don't consume that income, they save it or pay it in taxes. Firms plan for investment, but it may or may not be equal to what people save. And what the government spends may not be equal to what they take in through taxation. Still, it all has to add up in the end. If savings are more than firms want to invest—that is, if consumption is not as high as firms planned—build-ups in inventories will affect future production decisions. If taxes fall short of government spending, the government must sell bonds that compete with and can impact private sector bonds. A disturbance in consumption is usually compensated for by a change in savings. An increase in government bond sales may decrease the investment made by the private sector. Equilibrium means that as changes become evident in one sector of the economy, there will be compensating changes elsewhere.

CHAPTER 9

Real Estate: Is It Still Location, Location, Location?

One of the first activities attributed to humanoids, even before spoken languages, was to seek shelter. Our quest for cover is as old as fire. We simply don't like being exposed to the elements. Evolving in fits and starts over the millennia, that need is reflected today in construction techniques and property rights and other efforts and issues, some only marginally more sophisticated than contesting for and settling into the most comfortable cave.

The basics of sheltering have changed little. If you don't have more people, you don't need more shelter. But with an influx of people, shelter can be at a premium and you might have to compete for it. These days we worry about homeless people because all sorts of bad things—disease, accidents, violence—can happen as a consequence of being exposed. And beyond mere comfort and safety, having a place to live, an address, is essential to securing employment as well as accumulating possessions and wealth.

Commercial real estate is much the same. Business-related shelter is as essential as having a roof over your family's head. Keeping business activity out of the elements allows for much improved outcomes—aside from landscapers, construction sites, and football teams (and even they need indoor spaces for planning and operations). There are practical reasons for gathering in one place to conduct business, for workers to be collaborating within the confines of an office building or a manufacturing facility, even if COVID-19 called into question where some of us work most productively. Do professional services need to be performed behind a closed door on the 23rd floor of a New York skyscraper with a view of downtown Manhattan, or could some professionals work just as effectively at home in their basements? Some basic questions about the organizational work-place are being asked that have significant implications for residential as well as commercial real estate.

People Follow Jobs and Quality of Life

Owning a home was long thought fundamental to living the American Dream, though that concept took a beating during the Great Recession. Financial consultants changed their characterization of a house as most peoples' "largest single asset and biggest source of wealth" to "biggest single item on their balance sheet." Home ownership was restoring its reputation and appeal as we moved through the twenty-teens, and it is clear that owning a home is potentially a huge source of wealth, if not income. An enormous amount of peoples' personal wealth is wrapped up homes.

Single-family residential real estate is driven by two factors: where people want to live and household formation in the economy. If you have a high birth rate, you eventually need places for all those people. Aggregate housing starts should more or less match-up with growth in the number of households, with the exception of some adjustments, such as migration, which requires more housing and therefore more construction in a particular area, even if the overall population is unchanged. As well, we see that growth in the number of households ebbs and flows with the maturation of generations of baby booms and baby busts.

It is easy to misinterpret the relationship between the stock of real estate and the GDP accounts. While real estate represents an enormous amount of wealth, that wealth by itself does not contribute to nor is it necessarily a sign of a healthy GDP. A great deal of activity around real estate generates income—lenders, lawyers, real estate managers—but not real estate itself. Construction, the addition to the stock of real estate, is the investment activity that adds to GDP.

Still, the existing stock of real estate helps us make predictions about GDP investment in the context of the larger economy. We pay very close attention to economic indicators like new housing starts, building permits, and groundbreaking announcements by construction firms. They tell us a great deal about the near-term construction impact on GDP, and also about what the business community thinks the future is going to look like and where people are going to live and work.

An Emerging Sun Belt

If you don't like cold weather and you're looking for a job, you're likely to look in a warmer climate. So we've seen a great deal of construction in the Sun Belt, which combines warmer weather and a lower cost of living to attract more residents and workers. North Carolina and Michigan illustrate the point. They are comparable in terms of population, slightly more than 10 million each in 2019. But North Carolina employed 231,500 construction workers that year to Michigan's 173,400, about a third more. North Carolina is typical of Sun Belt states, which are consistently recording above national average economic growth.

Where you decide to live is function of lifestyle and what you can afford given your employment. That has made the Sun Belt the fastest growing section of the United States. Employers have followed suit, moving their companies to where they can get the best workers for the wages they offer. Houston, Atlanta, Charlotte, Raleigh, Nashville, Dallas, Orlando, Tampa: These cities are attracting waves of workers, including new college and advanced-degree graduates with knowledge critical to twenty-first century employers. It is no wonder their companies and jobs are following the graduates.

From an equilibrium perspective, residential housing and commercial real estate need to be developed more or less simultaneously. People need places to both live and work. So while we tend to look at residential and commercial real estate separately in assessing our economy, what drives each market is not all that different. Some states, like Florida, have tried to focus on attracting retirees where the migrants weren't looking for industrial or office space. But in general the demand for real estate is about both living and working—which takes us back to real estate and investing in real estate being all about figuring out where people want to spend their lives.

Takeaways

- One of the human race's first needs was for shelter, and over the millennia that has translated into an enormous amount of wealth being wrapped up in homes and commercial buildings.

- People and businesses locate where they believe their lifestyle and business prospects will be best, which has made the Sun Belt, due to weather and affordability, the fastest growing section of the United States.
- Real estate and investing in real estate are about figuring out where people want to live and work, and the results show up in the construction portion of GDP.

Equilibrium

Real estate is one of the most essential markets in the economy; it is where we live and work. Consequently, watching trends unfold in real estate can tell us a lot about the economy. It's "location, location, location." If no one wants to live or work in a particular place, real estate in that place won't be worth much. Conversely, a highly desirable location will be highly valued. What constitutes a desirable location changes over time with differing social preferences and changing technology. Air conditioning was essential for populating the U.S. Sun Belt, and the ease of long-distance travel has made more locations feasible for living and working globally. The wealth represented by the stock of real estate is a major part of many individuals' investment portfolios, and the investment in new construction is a notable contributor to GDP.

CHAPTER 10

Lighten Up: Capital Expenditure and Intellectual Property

When did interactive video games morph from a pastime that angered parents to a lucrative profession? Maybe if you were good at Space Invaders or Ms. Pacman, someone might buy you a beer, but today, professional video gaming is a huge global industry. Esports teams from Korea to France, in India and the United States compete around the world in games like League of Legends, CS: GO, Hearthstone, Super Smash Bros., Overwatch, Dota 2, Rocket League, Fortnite, PUBG, StarCraft II, and Call of Duty. When the league around the game Overwatch announced it would add teams, communications giant Cox and a partner paid an estimated $30–$60 million to get Atlanta into the first expansion round. Video gaming is not only a competitive sport but has also become, as a GDP category, a huge investment of human capital.

GDP is getting lighter. So Alan Greenspan often asserted even before he became chairman of the Federal Reserve in 1987. It sometimes struck his audiences as an odd topic, but it was an astute observation with broad implications for the economy. Long ago, the architect and futurist Buckminster Fuller, who designed the Geodesic Dome, predicted that people would one day assess buildings in terms of what they weighed as opposed to what they cost. There was something to be said for efficient design and the economic use of materials, but Greenspan understood that manufacturing, which for years had been the focal point for expanding GDP, particularly in developing economies, was becoming a less critical part of national and global economies. No longer could we measure the advance of our economy by heavy industry. "Building" intellectual property was becoming and is now a dominant source of economic growth.

Big Payoffs: Intellectual Property

We used to think of investment as limited to tangible goods, equipment more than anything, but also real estate. While those still command a significant portion of GDP, today the big payoffs for investors are generated by intellectual property. Innovation has allowed for the monetization of intellectual property and that has accounted for enormous revenue streams across the globe and in all segments of the economy. The development of vaccines for the COVID-19 virus illustrated the level of commitment of both public and private investment to innovation and intellectual property. While the vaccine itself is produced in physical-capital-intensive labs, the process of developing the vaccine required a huge amount of human capital: the training and experience of the medical scientists developing the drugs. We do heavy industry well, but whether it's medicine or software or the code that moves a vehicle forward autonomously, the value-add to GDP today—and far into the future—is more and more in intellectual property.

That isn't to say that investment in plant equipment is irrelevant. On the contrary, in almost all cases when intellectual property finds value, it is manifested in some process that requires physical production. But there are an increasing number of cases where that is not true, as in some creative arts, like live concerts, which are performed largely using existing infrastructure and capital. Or in esports that feature competition over an existing Internet infrastructure. Or by TV and movie producers who use existing protocols and hardware to transmit their creations.

Measuring Intellectual Property for GDP

Investment in intellectual property is more difficult to define and categorize than investment in heavy industry where you get to see the new machinery on the factory floor. If you work in research in a factory, you work to make a product better. The Thomas Edison Research Laboratory was all about new products and new uses for physical materials—rubber, for example—where the end product was something tangible. Today an increasing share of research is about investing in and developing human capital, which, in turn, will be better able to develop more intellectual property.

Consider the artist, one who draws or paints on a canvas. She might redirect her talent, along with learning something of engineering, to draw buildings that are realistic and functional. The artist becomes architect. We think of architects as pursuing a different kind of education than a fine arts degree, but the creativity involved in putting something completely new on paper or a digital device does not differ so greatly between the two.

Take it a step further: Instead of architects who build buildings, we have architects that build microchips, a skill we typically think of as part of an electrical engineering education. But it is also about placing little bitty components in the same way an architect thinks about placing bigger components and the same way a painter puts objects into a painting. On some level, the creative processes aren't that different, even if the specialized field behind each is. Technical and artistic creativity are related, which also makes the idea of investing in creative human capital harder to define and categorize.

Intellectual property is much more fungible than heavy industry. It is without mass, which has profound implications on where it can be produced, how it can be produced, where it can be marketed and applied. A virtual reality work has to accurately render what people look like and how they behave and move, so we have a great melding of what we had in the past. What we thought of as purely creative art now has another outlet of value in the economy. The human capital that is associated with and facilitates certain kinds of creativity is now something pushing economic growth. The line between investment that enhances GDP and a purely artistic effort that might have some economic value but is not initially intended to produce GDP is no longer so clear.

As the economy gets more complex and as technology progresses, it becomes quite clear that the investment in physical and human capital is more integrated, the confusion between creativity and some commercial endeavor is much more blurred. Intellectual property is a powerful force moving the global economy forward. We're still making a lot of money building buildings, but more and more returns are coming from ideas that can power innovation.

Fungible and Challenging

The ease with which intellectual property can move around, including across borders, presents its own challenges. International trade disputes often center around intellectual property, its protection and use. The concept of "nothing new under the sun" has morphed to be about how innovations are frequently combinations and permutations of existing ideas.

We use patents and copyrights to protect intellectual property. But detecting infringement is often easier when it involves a physical product. How an innovation separates two pieces of intellectual property with little physical manifestation is more complicated. Accounting software does arithmetic, and all arithmetic will lead to the same result. When does one piece of accounting software infringe on another when their basic functions are essentially identical? How do you distinguish between reusing ideas as opposed to stealing ideas?

Such challenges to investing in intellectual property continue to grow in number and complexity. How much of a particular innovation is really new and what is a twist on an existing idea? These are difficult social, legal, and economic issues, as tough as measuring intellectual property investment and output for GDP.

Takeaways

- GDP is getting lighter.
- Video gaming is not only a competitive sport, it has become, as a GDP category, a huge investment of human capital.
- Technical and artistic creativity are not so loosely related, which also makes the idea of investing in creative human capital harder to define and categorize.
- The line between investment that enhances GDP and a purely artistic effort that might have some economic value but is not initially intended to produce GDP is not so clear.

- International trade disputes often center around intellectual property, its protection, and use.
- How do you distinguish between reusing ideas and stealing ideas?

Equilibrium

Technology and the fruits of investment have evolved dramatically over time and as resources get reallocated. Innovations we think of as entertainment also have applications that go well beyond entertaining. The same kind of coding that allows you to control a 3-D virtual character might also be applicable in a medical application. The principle of equilibrium is evidenced in the interconnectedness of investments and the mechanisms by which information investment diffuses itself and gets applied in potentially unexpected ways to produce better outcomes.

CHAPTER 11

Inventories: The Buffer between Production and Consumption

When a consumer or company buys something, the seller has three ways to meet the requirements of the purchase.

First, the seller can make the purchased item on the spot, a particularly common practice for service providers. Many services—haircuts, personal training, restaurant dining—are personal in nature; providing and producing the service are the same thing. You can't perform a haircut at a time different from when the consumer is sitting in the chair.

Not all services require such immediacy. If you have your tax return done by an accountant, there is a period of time between when you hand over your documents and you are told how much you owe the Internal Revenue Service. The accounting firm doesn't have an inventory of tax returns to pull off the shelf; there's a buffer between the time you engage the accountant and the time the service is produced.

A second way to deliver goods is to take them out of inventory, which is typically what happens when we buy a product. When you buy carrots at the grocery store you draw down on the store's carrot inventory. When you buy a car from a dealership, you buy it out of dealer inventory. Again there are exceptions, such as products on a retailer's shelves there by consignment, where the retailer doesn't contractually take possession of the product from the manufacturer until it is sold. (It comes out of the manufacturer's inventory that happens to be kept on store shelves.) But no matter the accounting arrangement, when you purchase something material, it is usually done by drawing down from inventory somewhere.

A third option for providing goods or services, at least as far as the national income accounts are concerned, is to import your purchase.

There are accounting nuances, but obtaining your purchase directly from abroad doesn't add to GDP—it's not "domestic." Consumption rises by the amount of your purchase and the net trade balance declines by the same amount, leaving the GDP unchanged.

So inventories can generally be thought of as the buffer between production and consumption. If you want carrots today, the provider had to anticipate your purchase far enough in advance to get carrots from a farm to your grocery cart. You can't schedule the production of crops to coincide with the consumption of produce.

In our reference in Chapter 4 to the run on toilet paper at the outset of the COVID-19 pandemic—it happened again as cases soared in the fall of 2020—we noted that people built up inventories at home and depleted stores' inventories. We don't count the extra toilet paper at home as an inventory investment—for the sake of GDP, it is personal consumption—but in principle, that's what it is. Retailers had to scramble for more product, upsetting the usual balance in the toilet paper supply chain by the relocation of where the inventories of toilet paper were being held (or hoarded).

JIT Management and Inventory

Agriculture paints a clear picture of the role inventories play, but they are also critical to manufacturing. You could say that inventories make modern production and modern business commerce possible. As buffers at various stages of the manufacturing process, they are critical because deliveries of intermediate goods through the supply chain don't always coincide with the production schedule of the final good. Manufacturers are often saddled with large, idle inventories of intermediate goods at their manufacturing sites awaiting use in the production process. It's necessary; inventories are required to produce in a timely manner. They are expensive to hold and manage, but not as expensive as having to stop production because the factory has run out of some intermediate input.

Just-in-time (JIT) production and management, delivering something just as it is needed, illustrates the duality of the relationship between inventory and supply chain management. It has extended the concept of inventory from something in the warehouse to include something on a boat to be delivered to a warehouse. When it was introduced to the world in the 1960s by Japan, and in particular Toyota, it was hailed as a game-changing cost-saving innovation. No longer would a manufacturer have to maintain huge inventories of parts.

JIT management and the associated advances in tracking technology have allowed us to consider inventory, supply chain, and logistics as an integrated system. But even as inventory and supply chain management have become more sophisticated, inventory has maintained its role as a buffer in the production and consumption processes.

Inventory Management

A business can fail if consumers decide not to buy an item it has produced. But from a macroeconomic perspective, a bigger problem is when consumers decide not to buy as much across the entire economy as they did previously, when they decide instead to save. When consumers pull back in a systematic way across the economy and don't buy the products that have been produced, producers won't need to make as much in the subsequent economic period. Nor will they need as many employees.

One of John Maynard Keynes' major contributions to economics literature was his observation that the decision to save was not the same as the decision to invest. That is, planned saving may not be the same as planned investment. If consumers decide to consume less of current production and save more, inventories of unsold production will build up—and to the detriment of the economy.

Prior to Keynes, these production imbalances were thought to be mostly transitory. A producer simply made a mistake in assessing what people wanted and would take a loss. But that was idiosyncratic and the markets would adjust. Keynes saw that systemic increases in savings in the economy—people might increase savings in fear of a coming recession—and the resulting increase in inventories would drive down production which would, in turn, drive down income. In the long term, that vicious circle could result in a recession; the expectation of the recession could cause the recession. And inventories, specifically the unplanned buildup of inventories, would be a central player in the process.

Many economists believe we've had fewer recessions over the last few decades because we've evolved to a more service-oriented economy. Physical inventories dwindled in importance to the overall economic scheme as they became a smaller share of the economy. Mistakes producers of goods make relative to overproduction have less impact on the economy when most of what consumers buy is made on demand. Production mistakes can still occur in a service economy, but those mistakes will show up as idle capacity—empty barber chairs—and not an excess of physical goods in stock. Still, unintended excess inventory is one of the most closely monitored economic signals. Even though it does not impact GDP as much as it used to, the fluctuation in business inventories indicates potential mismatches that could deliver an economic slowdown.

Using inventory changes as an economic forecasting tool is complicated by two factors causing changes in inventory, one bad and one good. It's bad if you've manufactured more product than people want to buy and are stuck with unintended inventory. But building up inventories is good if the economy looks like it's going to take off, and you are making product in anticipation of demand. If you are a builder and don't have an inventory of building materials, you can't build houses. So if you expect a brisk housing market, as it was in 2020 during the COVID-19 pandemic when many people moved from community style housing to single-family dwellings, you build up your inventory of materials. On the other hand, if you pile up materials and the housing market slows, the unintended excess inventory can deal your construction business, and your suppliers, a serious blow. The increased demand combined with tariffs on imported lumber virtually doubled lumber prices between April and October 2020. How much lumber inventory should a contractor buy at those prices? How much more would their customers be willing to pay for a home improvement?

Watching inventories as a signal of what's happening in an economy is important but tricky. In both good and bad cases, the buildup is an investment that adds to GDP. In the short run, whether firms are right or wrong in their production decisions, an increase in inventories will get you a higher GDP figure than you would have without it. The question is what will happen in the next quarter.

Takeaways

- Changes in inventory provide a significant signal about the future of the economy, but whether they signal good or bad times is not always immediately evident.
- Because of a steady increase in the service sector of the economy as a percentage of GDP, material inventories don't play as large a role as they did in previous decades.
- Inventories also serve as a buffer between domestic producers and intermediate goods producers, so inventories also have implications for the overall supply chain process, and particularly international trade, as we will see in our chapters on trade.

Equilibrium

Inventories are a spot-on example of equilibrium as macroeconomists understand it. You conceive of the change in inventories as a buffer between the demand and supply sides of the economy, and use that calculation to make an observation about the economy going forward. Changes in inventories must match up with changes in production and consumption, and the difference between what is produced and consumed is a change in inventory. That is the mechanical aspect of inventory, and understanding the reason for the change is key to understanding the balance between future production and consumption.

CHAPTER 12

State and Local Governments: Where Spending Gets Done

COVID-19 was a large-scale natural disaster, global in scope. When natural disasters strike in the United States, the federal government deploys coping and relief mechanisms, including the Federal Emergency Management Association (FEMA), to deal with the consequences and aid in the physical and economic restoration of the affected areas. They work a lot like insurance. When the Gulf Coast is hit by a hurricane, tornadoes wreak havoc in the Midwest or wildfires ravage the West, the whole nation kicks in to help the affected area in its recovery. But the pandemic was an unprecedented natural disaster. It affected the entire country, and rather uniformly, and the concept of insurance, all to the aid of one, does not work well when all are in need.

Or when the need is global. Australia sent firefighters to California to help control the 2020 blazes and U.S. workers went to Haiti in 2010 to help in the aftermath of the earthquake. But cross-national aid wasn't available during the pandemic; there were essentially no unused resources globally.

While the traditional means for coping with natural disasters in the United States were not applicable or available, the need for aid still existed. Most of the burden for dealing with COVID-19 fell to state and local governments and their public safety and public health departments. The expense was overwhelming: dramatically increased costs not only for healthcare related services but for law enforcement, the judiciary and schools. And as is always the case with natural disasters, the pain was worst in the most resource-constrained districts.

State and local governments struggled to mount a defense. As with any natural disaster, the local government is the first responder.

When responding overwhelms a locality, the federal government steps in, typically as FEMA, to coordinate the movement of resources to the affected area from unaffected areas. But in this case, the needs were too widespread and resources scarce. As well, in light of the pandemic-associated recession, the usual sources of funding for state and local governments, taxes, dwindled as the demands for the services they provide increased.

Where's the Money?

When we talk about government spending, we naturally think about the federal government because its budget is so large—and because we pay the majority of our taxes to the federal government. But outside of military and some infrastructure projects, most of our federal tax money gets transferred out of the federal government before it shows up in GDP accounts. That is, while the federal government spends a lot of money, it is not directly consuming goods and services, even though it could be financing those purchases by some other entity. In terms of direct spending, about 60 percent of government's contribution in the United States to GDP occurs at state and local levels. State and local governments are all about consumption, providing for public schools, public safety, and infrastructure. State and local governments are where the action is, where spending gets done.

That can get tricky in bad times. Unlike the federal government, state and local governments can't run deficits. They have to balance their budgets; they can't borrow money to finance ongoing operating deficits. They can issue debt to fund capital projects, but that debt typically is financed by related income streams—a school bond, for example, paid for by a property tax increase. But because they cannot borrow to pay for the routine services they provide, they face a particularly difficult fiscal challenge when the economy turns sour.

Sources and Surpluses

State and local governments get revenue from three sources: sales and use taxes, income taxes (in most states), and property taxes—some state and local governments have other idiosyncratic revenue sources, for example, government-owned conference facilities. During a recession, sales and income taxes decline, even as the demand for public services increases; public safety and education don't respond to the business cycle—or if they do, the demand for their services does not decline. One frequent lament of technical and community college presidents is that enrollment increases when there is a downturn in the economy. Overvalued property was a feature of the 2008 recession; as property valuations declined, so did property taxes, leaving state and local governments with losses in all three of their main sources of income.

States prepare for times of need by stockpiling surpluses, so-called rainy day funds. But that process is idiosyncratic. Some states do well; others not so well. When a state comes up short, it's usually not due to a lack of oversight by a current administration, just a function of how, over many of its administrations, the state approaches providing for hard times.

Declining property values were in large part responsible for a slower recovery from the 2008 recession than some analysts might have expected. When the private sector of the economy finally did turn around, property valuations continued to be marked down, and the decline took more than three years to be fully reflected in property tax revenues. Public services that depended on property taxes were short of needed funding well into the private sector recovery.

The inability to borrow to sustain operations is only one of many factors that put state and local governments on different footing than the federal government. But those distinctions are hard to appreciate when times are tough and citizens need more government services. Because it can finance deficits, the federal government often comes to the aid of a state or locality. But in the case of COVID-19, the federal government's response was uneven and did not result in timely aid as the administration and Congress haggled over which states needed money and when.

Takeaways

- About 60 percent of government activity in the U.S. economy occurs at state and local levels.

- The demand for state and local government services increases when the economy slows and that's the time when state and local governments are most squeezed.
- Unlike the federal government, states cannot routinely engage in deficit spending.
- State and local governments have rainy day funds but they all do it differently: some well, some not so well.
- The federal government has programs, including FEMA, for providing aid to areas of the country recovering from a natural disaster. But COVID-19 affected the entire country and rather uniformly, so the usual formula of many coming to the aid of one was inapplicable.

Equilibrium

When we think about government spending, we reflexively think of the federal government because of its size and pervasive national influence. But state and local governments are all about consuming the goods and services needed to provide the most fundamental government support. When disaster strikes, localities often rely on the federal government to provide relief by transferring resources from areas unaffected by the disaster. But that give-and-take formula can prove insufficient when disaster strikes the entire economy.

CHAPTER 13

Stabilization and Procyclicality: How Governments Balance Spending with Taxes

One of governments' roles in society, one of their primary roles, is to keep things going, to stabilize their economy with measures that provide relief, such as a stimulus, during a downturn. In economic terms, federal, state, and local governments should be countercyclical in their spending and policies. Of course, that doesn't always happen because their revenue streams are procyclical. When the economy sours, tax revenues decline, and that makes it harder for governments to engage in their usual activities, to provide services as they would normally, even without additional programs to stimulate the economy.

For the U.S. government, an economic downturn might call for aggressive countercyclical measures financed by deficit spending. But state and local governments generally don't have that option. As we have noted, state and local governments typically can't run deficits to pay for routine operations, can't issue loans to finance operating deficits, and have to balance their budgets. That creates an enormous challenge in a downturn as they are called upon to provide more social services but have less money to do so because of declining tax revenues. So they often wind up cutting back on services and adding to the downturn. To provide, at a minimum, the services they offered before the downturn, they turn to the federal government.

But if the federal policymakers don't want to add to the federal debt, the local policymakers must find places to make spending cuts to have the funds to help with relief. However, if they cut, say, military spending, the communities that depend on military spending suffer. At state and local levels, where deficit financing is not an option, do you pull resources from schools so you don't have to make cuts to public safety? Or cut back on police and fire department funding to keep educational systems functioning? Do you change the conditions under which you deliver state-provided health care? And how will it be restored? Balancing what needs to be done across the board is complex. There are myriad difficult issues, considerations and moving parts—and the decisions often have to be made under conditions of great uncertainty.

Automatic Stabilizers

The federal government has policies in place to "automatically" stabilize an economic downturn or at least dampen its effects. The two main automatic stabilizers:

- A progressive tax code. The higher your income, the higher share of your income you pay in taxes. If your income declines, so does your tax burden or tax rate, a sort of built-in tax cut. During an economic downturn, a progressive tax code translates to disproportionately lower tax collections, the goal being to stabilize disposable income.
- Unemployment compensation. Workers who have lost their jobs receive relief in the form of weekly unemployment compensation payments. States build up balances in unemployment insurance funds to cover possible downturns, and if those balances are insufficient, the states essentially borrow money from the federal government to make the payments, then pay it back when their economies improve. It is a collaborative effort. State labor departments manage the programs and get the funds to repay the federal government mainly from employers whose payments are adjusted according to their experience in terms of layoffs and furloughs.

The stabilizers are considered automatic because policymakers don't have to pass legislation or take other actions to implement them. As such the relief is more immediate, and avoids the lags inherent in policymaking.

Policy Lags

Even if policymakers agree that steps should be taken to stimulate the economy, there are unavoidable lags in getting programs functioning. These lags fall into two classes:

- Inside lags happen during the policymaking process. Recognition lags occur because it can be difficult for policymakers to determine that a recession is upon us. Recessions usually occur when there is a downturn in one segment of the economy that spreads to others; it is not always apparent where the tipping point is. Nor are recessions evenly spread across the country. Policymakers get different assessments from different constituencies.
- Another type of inside lag relates to implementation. Even when lawmakers generally agree the country is in a recession, it takes time to agree on what to do about it. The legislative process can be time-consuming. Programs that involve new government efforts take time to organize.
- Outside lags. Outside lags are the result of the time it takes the policy, once implemented, to have an effect on the economy. During the COVID-19 recession, the federal government issued checks to citizens based on their incomes as reported on their previous year's income tax returns. The payments' effects were felt immediately; people spent the checks soon after they arrived. The outside lag was short. The federal government might respond to a slowdown with a tax cut to stimulate business activity and get the country out of recession. It might work, but there will likely be a lengthy lag from the time the tax cut is implemented to when the cut is analyzed by the private sector to determine appropriate spending and investment responses, to when those spending and investment responses are executed, to when those changes actually stimulate the economy.

Apart from lags, a stimulus can have unintended consequences. Consider that tax cut. It might help some industries more than others, which might not have been the intent. It could change the interactions among different sectors of the economy, particularly with their foreign counterparts. It might not accomplish what it set out to do. Measuring the effectiveness as well as the impact of a tax cut can take years before the data is definitive.

In 2001, the recession was relatively shallow and relatively short. Had a tax cut been policymakers' response, by the time inside and outside lags had transpired and the stimulus showed up, the recession would have been over. That's one problem with countercyclical policy; given the lags, the problems can disappear—and almost certainly will change—before the solutions arrive. You can add to the national debt unnecessarily when your actions take so long to take effect.

Now consider The America Recovery and Reinvestment Act of 2009. The initial data presented to policymakers underestimated the depth of the so-called Great Recession. Policymakers were eager to act with minimal lags, but the data they were working with was eventually revised to reveal a much more severe downturn than they initially thought.

In the case of the initial COVID-19 stimulus checks, it was clear they were needed. But it was not so clear what was needed in a second round. Some people legitimately, even desperately, needed help, but other sectors of the economy were doing well. Congressional leaders argued over what kind of relief and how much was appropriate, which led to an extended inside lag.

Inside lags at the state level can be meaningful, substantially exacerbating an already problematic environment. Many states don't have full-time legislators or single-year budgets. That makes it extremely difficult to respond to an economic downturn in a timely way. Without federal support the state might have to cut spending. But where? If the legislature is not in session, gearing up for another budget session can be time-consuming. The Georgia state legislature meets for a short session at beginning of the calendar year, and begins work on its budget early the preceding fall. Texas' budget is set for a two-year period, a comparatively long time for spending commitments to be in place requiring a more involved process to rebalance them. Even California and New York with full-time legislatures are slowed by institutional features that can delay their response to sudden disasters.

Takeaways

- Government revenue is procyclical; we would like government spending to be countercyclical.
- Balancing what needs to be cut in an economic downturn in order to provide basic services is a challenge for state and local governments that cannot rely on deficit spending.
- The federal government has two automatic stabilizers in place to deal with economic downturns: a progressive tax code and unemployment compensation.
- Two types of lags slow relief to people in need: inside lags, the time it takes to determine there is a need to develop a policy, and outside lags, the time it takes to implement the policy.

Equilibrium

In times of economic distress we typically might look to government for relief, but the same conditions that are causing people's incomes to decline are causing governments' incomes to decline. No one is immune to a business cycle and creating appropriate policies to manage that cycle is harder than it might appear at first glance. At the state and local level there are limited options, and at the federal level an assortment of lags may hinder a timely policy response.

CHAPTER 14

Federal Spending: Budgets and Deficit Spending

People love to debate federal fiscal policy, setting the "correct" level of taxation and spending and the resulting federal deficit and debt. But in arguing they need to be careful about the often-confused distinction between deficit and debt. They are different and the distinction is important. The deficit is the *change* in outstanding debt; the sum of all past deficits is the *amount* of outstanding debt. The U.S. federal deficit for fiscal 2020 was $3.1 trillion; the outstanding debt held by the public at the end of August 2020 was $20.8 trillion (source: U.S. Treasury Department).

Unlike the debt, which is a fairly uncomplicated concept, understanding the deficit is not as simple as looking at an accounting entry. There are two basic and related federal deficit formats: the deficit that is commonly reported and the primary deficit. The reported deficit is the amount the government needs to finance to accommodate the difference between what it takes in through taxation and the total amount it spends. The primary deficit, however, is the difference between the tax revenues the government takes in and what it spends on the various programs it has decided to fund—that is, the reported deficit minus the spending to service the accumulated outstanding debt.

Policymakers get to manage the primary deficit. Changes in tax policy change the amount of revenue taken in and thus the primary deficit. As well, they can make changes in spending on programs that will raise or lower the primary deficit. The difference between the primary deficit and the deficit that gets reported is the debt service on outstanding debt. Debt service is something policymakers have little to no control over.

The outstanding debt represents the historical accumulation of federal deficits. It was sold at certain interest rates and under certain terms and conditions that require it to be serviced. Current policymakers must accommodate the debt service, even if it is a burden they inherited, not of their making. Short of repudiating the debt, they are stuck with whatever spending is needed to support the outstanding obligations.

The reported deficit is, then, the combination of the primary deficit and the amount of interest due on the built up debt incurred in previous years and administrations.

Where there is no outstanding debt, primary and reported deficits are the same. But if you have outstanding debt and want to zero out the reported deficit, or at least start eating away at it, you have to bring in more tax revenue than you spend on programs by an amount greater than the debt service. That is, the primary budget must be in surplus sufficiently to offset the debt service requirements.

Balanced Budgets

From a political perspective, an administration promising to balance the budget will have to take in taxes equal to what it will spend on programs and debt service combined. Of course, spending on current programs is a greater priority for a current administration over spending to support the debt built up from previous administrations' programs. Tax cuts or spending increases are much more fun to announce than austerity measures. Still, if you're going to balance the budget, debt service must be paid; it takes priority.

Budget balances are a thorny issue not because governments can't run deficits but as debt accumulates, it imposes greater restrictions on what the current administration can do with tax revenue. Every dollar of debt service is one less dollar that can be dedicated to building roads or exploring space—unless policymakers agree to increase the deficit or raise taxes.

Even the massive amount of $20.8 trillion in outstanding debt reported at the end of 2020 is not much of a hardship for the United States (though that is debatable depending on perspective and estimates of future economic performance). But countries with demonstrable debt crises must match current spending, including debt service, with revenue.

They simply can't borrow more money. Even outside of a debt crisis, borrowing more to service outstanding debt can make for dynamic instability, and a large amount of current outstanding debt is a real concern if you are considering policies that would create additional debt.

One response to dynamic instability is to call for a continuously balanced budget, as in a balanced budget amendment to the constitution, which deprives policymakers the option of deliberate deficit spending. But that imposes artificial constraints on the current government. In a time of recession when revenues are in decline, cutting spending to match the decline in tax revenue is hardly appropriate. When the economy is struggling, the federal government should be able to step in, run a deficit and return the economy closer to full employment.

Debt to GDP

It isn't enough to talk only about the size of the debt but to scale it to the economy, the ratio of debt to GDP. In 2020, the U.S. deficit was more than three times that of 2019, but we were besieged by a pandemic costing governments at all levels both in lost tax revenues and forced spending. If it was time after the pandemic to reign in the deficits, it was also important to consider the size of the deficit and debt compared to GDP. At the end of 2020, the U.S. debt-to-GDP ratio was about where it was at end of World War II (See Figure 14.1), and at a little over one-to-one not historically out of balance or overly concerning. Japan's debt-to-GDP ratio in 2020 was more than three to one, apparently not considered problematic by financial markets as Japan had no problem selling their sovereign debt.

Nor would such levels of debt be considered alarming for an individual. When you build a house, you can take on a mortgage of about three times your income. Maybe that's not the best way to think about sovereign debt, but it is an argument often made: people run higher debt-to-income ratios than the federal government. And, the argument goes, the sovereign is able to maintain a higher ratio than an individual due to, among other things, its longer life expectancy, its ability to tax, and its ability to issue money.

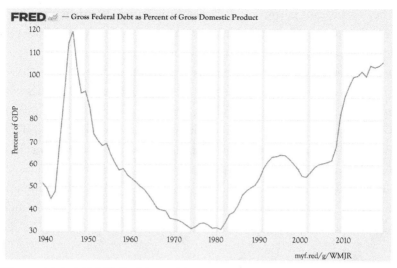

Figure 14.1 2020 U.S. debt-to-GDP ratio similar to end of World War II

Source: Federal Reserve Bank of St. Louis

Source: U.S. Office of Management and Budget

Release: Debt to Gross Domestic Product Ratios

Units: Percent of GDP, Not Seasonally Adjusted

Frequency: Annual Gross Federal Debt as Percent of Gross Domestic Product (GFDGDPA188S) was first constructed by the Federal Reserve Bank of St. Louis in January 2013. It is calculated using Gross Federal Debt (FYGFD) and Gross Domestic Product (GDPA):GFDGDPA188S = (FYGFD/GDPA)*100

Federal Reserve Bank of St. Louis and U.S. Office of Management and Budget, Gross Federal Debt as Percent of Gross Domestic Product [GFDGDPA188S]. Retrieved from FRED, Federal Reserve Bank of St. Louis; https://fred.stlouisfed.org/series/GFDGDPA188S,

October 15, 2020.

Cyclically Balanced Budgets

There's nothing magical about a calendar year in terms of budgeting, but if you think budgets should balance, they certainly don't day to day, given the randomness of tax receipts and spending. Many economists who argue for balanced budgets do so for a cyclically balanced budget, that is, over the course of a business cycle, through downturn and recovery. When times are bad the government can perform a valuable service by running deficits, then when the economy is doing well it should be running surpluses that pay down the debt. In any single year you would have variances, but over the course of a business cycle, good times surpluses would make up for bad times spending.

As we have noted, it is not always clear in real time when an economy is in a recession or recovery or how deep or superficial each is. Binding an administration to a balanced budget in an artificial 365-day period seems an undue burden. But even when you advocate longer-term balanced budgets, setting up the rules is tricky. You have to decide when to start diminishing deficits, that is when you think the economy is good enough and will remain good enough to begin running surpluses.

Time Inconsistency

A major problem facing policymakers is one that we are familiar with personally, the problem of time inconsistency in our preferences. Long-term commitments are difficult for policymakers—and people. The idea behind time-inconsistent preferences is that you might be better off doing something right now that you know you can't continue to do in the long run, like, "I'm going to eat this entire quart of ice cream." The optimal course is to do today what is unsustainable over time and commit to never doing it again, as in "I'll eat it tonight, but I'll never eat an entire quart of ice cream in one night again." The problem is that tomorrow you're faced with the same situation and the same choice as in, "Okay, just one more quart tonight, but for sure never again." The choice and decision logic are the same every night, so every night you eat the ice cream and every night you vow never to do it again. Time-inconsistent preference problems are everywhere. It's how bad reputations get made: you make promises that at some point in the future you won't want to keep, and not living up to your promises can have consequences.

Such behavior may be as pervasive in governmental fiscal policy as it is in society. As an elected policymaker you might have an incentive to do something you wouldn't agree to do over a long period. You might have inherited a balanced budget but you agree to aggressively spend to stimulate the economy and by stimulating the economy improve your chances of getting re-elected. And when you leave office, the burden of the debt you accumulated will pass to the next set of policymakers with the same incentives.

The Tax Cuts and Jobs Act of 2019 might prove an example of time-inconsistent policy. When Secretary of the Treasury Steven Mnuchin was asked why the administration would cut taxes amid record low employment, his answer was to stimulate the economy. But with close to full employment, and given the status of unemployment as a key economic indicator, was there a need to stimulate the economy? Economists generally agreed the United States didn't need tax cuts at that time.

In 2020, the United States had run large deficits that added to the federal debt, most resulting from the extraordinary strain on the economy from the COVID-19 pandemic. But there was no difficulty financing it, so little external pressure to generate primary budget surpluses to pay down debt. Still, the nagging question remained: when will we stop spending more money than we generate?

Takeaways

- The deficit is financed by *changing* the outstanding debt; if you sum up all the deficits you get the *amount* of outstanding debt.
- The reported deficit is a combination of the primary deficit and the amount of interest built up on the debt incurred in previous years and administrations.
- There is a great deal of focus on balancing budgets, for one reason, because additional debt restricts what the current administration can do with tax income.
- Many economists who argue for balanced budgets do so for a cyclically balanced budget, that is, over the course of a business cycle, through downturn and recovery.
- The idea behind time-inconsistent preferences is that you're better off doing something right now even if you think you can't continue to do in the long run—or don't know how long that long run is. This can be the case with government policies.

Equilibrium

Deficits and debt illustrate the dichotomy between short- and long-run equilibriums, particularly in a policy setting. What you want to do in the short term to maintain a healthy economy is maybe a good idea but by so doing you change the economic situation future policymakers will face and impose constraints on the economic choices they have.

CHAPTER 15

Jimmy Stewart, Oz, and the Road to a Federal Reserve

The conclusion of the Civil War found the nation's banks in as much disarray as the government. In the "free banking" era, which extended from about 1837 to the end of the War, there was no national guidance or control over lenders. Banks were organized at a state level with each state setting its own regulations. Many states and even banks issued their own currencies, much of which earned the nickname "shinplaster," the value of the notes being so little, their best use might be to cast a broken leg.

Such an unconnected financial system proved flimsy at best. Every four to eight years the nation would get caught up in financial panic. Runs on banks were, in a functional sense, closing down the economy. The banks' problems were rooted in "maturity transformation," where short-term liabilities, deposits, are used to fund long-term assets, loans. As illustrated so vividly by the movie *It's a Wonderful Life*, the two cease to cohabit comfortably when all of a bank's depositors want to withdraw all of their money at the same time. Without a Jimmy Stewart to explain to the townspeople that their money wasn't physically in the bank but in their homes and businesses, it was hard to stop a bank run. The bank was solvent in the sense that it had enough good assets to cover its liabilities. But the assets were long-term, the liabilities short-term, so when enough holders of the short-term liabilities converged on the bank, the bank faced a liquidity squeeze.

Most loans in those days were callable. The bank had a right to demand payment in full from the borrower at any time. And a bank run was one of those times. The problem would mushroom as one bank in trouble and calling loans put pressure on businesses to pay up, which put pressure on other businesses and people in debt to those businesses, which put pressure on other banks holding those debtors' deposits.

A bank experiencing a run might ask other banks for a loan based on its good, if long-term, loans. But this often didn't work. The solicitor would be turned down, not because the other banks were skeptical of the loans offered as collateral, but because they were concerned the panic might spread to them and therefore less willing to part with their own liquid assets.

The structure of banking in those days led to wholesale shutdowns, some widespread panics, and even recessions. Deposits weren't insured or in any way protected. Depositors in a bank without sufficient liquidity to offset a run forced their bank to liquidate otherwise good loans at fire-sale prices, turning a solvent institution insolvent. If you were a depositor, you'd end up losing your money—and that made for a greater, spreading panic.

The first-come, first-served nature of withdrawals rendered the panic perfectly reasonable from a depositor's perspective. If you weren't among the first in line, you ran the risk of not getting your money. Even if you thought the bank was well managed with a solid loan portfolio, it made sense to get in line at the first hint of trouble. The rational nature of the panic meant that even well-managed banks were subject to bank runs.

Metals or Promises

European countries with central banks to loan money to banks with collateral sufficient to satisfy depositors' demands didn't have this problem. But the concept of a central bank was not in favor in the United States. People feared bankers would control the economy, a paranoia that has been in play around the globe for thousands of years. Anti-central bank sentiment was one reason Alexander Hamilton was shot. Aaron Burr and Hamilton were on opposite sides of a debate regarding the establishment of a national bank: Hamilton in favor, Burr opposed. Of course, their disagreement was over more than the merits of a central bank. There was, however, one murder explicitly related: the shooting of a governor of New York City's Second National Bank—by a banker's son, no less.

The argument spawned the writing of what inadvertently became one of America's most beloved children's books and movies. The author of

The Wonderful Wizard of Oz, L. Frank Baum, a campaign worker for William Jennings Bryan, was an ardent supporter of a bi-metallic monetary standard. Baum and Bryan believed strongly that money should be backed by silver and gold. Hence, Dorothy's silver slippers (in the movie colorized to ruby) and the yellow (gold) brick road. Baum's book was allegory, the characters and scenes representing political figures and monetary concepts: the gold and silver taking Dorothy (the common person) to the Emerald City (greenbacks), Dorothy's return to Kansas where farmers would benefit from a monetary system that remained rooted in gold and silver, and so on.

The debate over whether currency should be backed by metals or other collateral carries on in one form or another. To this day, a considerable amount of anti-Federal Reserve sentiment exists.

The Panic of 1907, also known as the Knickerbocker Crisis, was a six-week stretch of runs on banks in New York City and other American cities in October and early November of that year. The 1906 San Francisco earthquake had so thoroughly devastated the city its reconstruction created a nationwide liquidity crunch that led to a recession. Panic swept the country and in every practical sense took down banking in the United States, leaving only a few banks in New York and Chicago as survivors. Those banks shared one characteristic: participation in clearinghouses.

Clearinghouses organized the exchange of checks or funds among member banks. At the end of each day, members gathered with their checks for a net settlement of what each bank owed or had coming. On days when there was too severe an imbalance in flows—for example, Morgan had a lot of checks written on it to Chase—then Chase would extend a credit to Morgan to manage the short-term imbalance. Morgan's was a liquidity problem, not a solvency problem. The clearinghouses were also charged with examining their members' books to ensure any short-term needs were only issues of liquidity, the examining committees' ultimate role being to ensure the member banks were—as bank examiners are charged with today—"safe and sound."

The Panic of 1907 awoke members of Congress to how well the clearinghouse model worked. They also noticed the role Europe's central banks played in preventing panics.

Evolving Solutions

In 1910, John Pierpont Morgan, Secretary of Treasury Henry Morganthau, and a handful of other financiers boarded a train for Jekyll Island, Georgia. To keep their intentions under wraps, they disguised the trip as a hunting party. But instead of tracking game, they gathered in a room at the Jekyll Island Resort and drafted a profile for a federal bank. When they emerged from what is still identified at the resort as the "Federal Reserve Room," they had a first draft of the bill Congress would pass to create the Federal Reserve System to clear checks, examine banks to ensure safe and sound lending practices, and extend short-term credit through a discount window that allowed banks to borrow against their good collateral to meet short-term liquidity needs. The Fed acted as a liquidity-providing backstop for the banking system; it was the "lender of last resort." The system didn't stop bank runs entirely, but it eliminated a major motive for "rational" panics.

The Great Depression of the late 1920s and early 1930s was spawned by a different source of bank failures, insolvency. The Fed was lending on sound loans, but many banks didn't have enough sound loans to cover depositors, so panic emerged again. The answer this time was the Federal Deposit Insurance Corporation (FDIC), established in 1933 under Franklin Roosevelt to ensure depositors access to up to $2,500 of their banked cash. The insurance would protect small depositors and remove their motive to run on a bank should the bank's solvency be in question. Deposit insurance, extended over time to the 2020 limit of $250,000, has worked to keep solvent banks in business.

In 2007 and 2008, the financial collapse was not about small depositors lining up to get their money, but about big depositors and their financial intermediaries, like Lehman Brothers, J.P. Morgan, and Goldman Sachs, which looked like banks but weren't—so-called non-bank banks. They were investment houses that managed funds that weren't insured by the FDIC. Portions of their portfolios were committed to investments like derivative securities on subprime mortgages. When the subprimes weren't paying off as expected and the securities derived from those loans didn't match their expected value, investors panicked, creating a liquidity crisis for those big institutions (in this case, the initial failing institutions were in Europe). Hence the downfall of uninsured Lehman Brothers and others. If your money was in a retail bank, you weren't particularly concerned—there were no Jimmy Stewart moments—but the big money was concerned and got pulled, and thus began two years of the so-called Great Recession.

Today the Federal Reserve System is comprised of twelve separate but interconnected banks and the Federal Reserve Board of Governors. By law, the Fed has a dual mandate: to maintain maximum employment and stable prices. In the late 1950s, the Fed worked in tandem with the Treasury on interest rates, but the partnership compromised the Fed's independence, leaving it vulnerable to the influence of the Treasury. Under the Eisenhower administration, the duties were segregated, leaving the Treasury responsible for the international value of the dollar and the Fed for interest rates. Still, the two are inextricably tied, just divided at a functional level.

In the 1950s Fed policy was driven by the so-called Phillips Curve, a theory that ties economic growth to inflation: growth generates more jobs and a tight labor market that leads to higher wages that result in inflation. Thus, the way to calm inflation is to have higher levels of unemployment. But the relationship was proven unreliable in the 1970s when fairly high inflation was accompanied by relatively high unemployment, and the Philips Curve was discredited for long-term use for monetary policy. As well, consider the years of increasingly declining unemployment rates and modest inflation following the Great Recession.

The Fed's dual mandate is a long-horizon mandate, sustainability and consistency over time, providing liquidity essentially through interest rate policy. So if the economy is not performing as well as it might, the Fed might ease lending conditions by lowering interest rates, but with a careful eye on the trade-off between inflation and unemployment. In the long run, stability seems to promote the best outcome.

Takeaways

- Central banks have played a dominant role in industrial economies for centuries, the United States being a little late in historical terms in getting one established.

- Since its inception, the Fed has provided greater, if far from perfect, stability to the economy, which, in turn, promotes long-term growth.
- The Fed is not always a popular institution. As noted by former Fed Chair William McChesney Martin, "It is the Fed's job to take the punch bowl away just as the party gets going."

Equilibrium

Central banks—in the United States, it is the Federal Reserve—are essential to the financial sector of most modern economies. Banks and many other financial intermediaries have an inherent potential problem with liquidity. They make money by taking in deposits and making loans. If depositors lose confidence in the lending decisions of the bank for whatever reason—a fear of an impending recession, a belief that the bank has lent too heavily in a sector of the economy that isn't doing well, or simply a line of depositors outside the bank wanting to withdraw their money and sparking rumors of a bank failure—it can result in a financial crisis wherein the banks cannot convert their solvent loans into cash fast enough to meet the demands of a bank run. Central banks serve as a "lender of last resort" that can step in to lend to stressed institutions, and provide sufficient liquidity to prevent a local problem from turning into a widespread crisis. The United States is historically skeptical of central banks, but persistent financial crises after the Civil War eventually led to the founding of the Federal Reserve System in 1913. Aside from trying to mitigate financial panics, the role of the Fed has gradually expanded to encompass a wide array of economic and social objectives.

CHAPTER 16

The Stop Sign (or Toll Booth) at the Border: Trade and Tariffs

When the United States placed tariffs on everything Chinese from minerals to handbags, China responded with tariffs on 128 U.S. products, from vegetables to whiskey to liquefied natural gas, from fruits and nuts to pork and soybeans. The battle escalated. Tariffs were extended to more goods on both sides and increased in severity from 10 to 25 percent. The trade war had massive repercussions around the world given those nations' status: China as the world's largest exporter and the United States as the world's largest importer—the two pillars of the global economy.

When Adam Smith wrote *Wealth of Nations*, the prevailing view on building a strong national economy was to run trade surpluses, limit imports, and pile up wealth in gold. He argued that true wealth is manifest in productive capacity, and ultimately, consumption. You can't eat gold; you eat bananas. He explained how open markets and free trade make both trading partners better off—if not, the exchange doesn't happen.

International commerce has always been the driver of civilization. Think Marco Polo, the merchant not the game. Seventeenth-century manufacturers and spice traders made Europe wealthier at a faster pace than the rest of the world. They could trade for spices and silks because of their relative advantage in basic manufactured goods, and their trading around the world made all nations participating in it better off. It was what powered Western civilization—in fact, the Silk Road provided, literally, a path for the development of civilization. The Ottoman Empire's dominance, nearly six centuries of it, is attributable to its geopolitically advantageous location for world trade.

Not much in this realm of thinking has changed since the seventeenth century and even less since Adam Smith's observations. The years have served to reinforce those foundational insights. Location might not be as important as it was for the Turks—maybe for a grocery store but not for a nation. What the United States had to sell, around the world as well as to its own citizens, is what made it the world's dominant economy.

Tariffs are the counterpoint to free trade: a stop sign at the border. Essentially, a tariff is a tax on an imported good. Tariffs are often implemented to intentionally raise the price of foreign goods to advantage domestic producers—and, consequently, disadvantage the domestic consumers who preferred to purchase the imported good.

There are a couple of appealing arguments for special cases where tariffs could be appropriate. For one, tariffs can protect a domestic industry that is emerging but not yet large enough to achieve the economies of scale in production that its foreign competitors enjoy. Another argument made by tariff proponents is that the protected industry serves some vital national interest that deserves the protection of the tax. In either case, tariffs are an easy way for governments to increase tax revenue.

Disruptions Have Consequences

Soybean growers in the Midwest have invested in expensive capital goods—tractors, planting devices, global positioning systems. Their investments, and the relatively fertile U.S. soil, have made them expert at growing soybeans. But the U.S.–China tariff war starting in 2018 effectively cut them off from their major customer. China wasn't importing soybeans as an act of goodwill. It needed soybeans to feed its people and their livestock, and the United States was an efficient producer compared to the rest of world.

There is historical precedence to consider. The Smoot-Hawley Tariff Act of 1930 had intended to protect U.S. farmers and manufacturers from cheap imports, but as other countries reacted with even steeper tariffs on U.S. exports the curtailment in international trade only served to expand and deepen the Great Depression. The results of protectionism are unambiguous: disrupt trade and both sides lose.

Consumer consumption accounts for in the neighborhood of 70 percent of the U.S. economy. Seventy percent of GDP is accounted for by people in America buying things, from cars to carrots. The U.S. and Chinese tariffs initially did little to derail consumption or affect most U.S. consumers. The impact was felt more on the production side of the U.S. economy: the makers of capital goods—cars, air conditioning units, microwaves, clothing—and intermediate goods, the products used to make capital goods, like steel and cotton. Because corporate income was relatively high at the inception of the tariffs, producers were able to absorb some of the impact. But when economic growth slows, consumers increasingly feel it.

As well-established economic relationships, particularly supply-chain connections, are disrupted, the results are predictable. The disruption in trade brought about by the 2018 and 2019 tariffs damaged China's economy; prices increased for Chinese consumers and farmers. At the same time, without the Chinese market, U.S. farmers watched prices for their harvested crops decline dramatically. The U.S. Court of Appeals for the Seventh Circuit, which includes Illinois, Indiana, and Wisconsin, received twice as many farm bankruptcy filings in 2018 as it did in 2008 at the height of the Great Recession. The U.S. Court of Appeals for the Eighth District—Iowa, Minnesota, Missouri, Arkansas, Nebraska, and North and South Dakota—handled a 96 percent increase in farm bankruptcy filings over the decade. And the U.S. Court of Appeals for the Tenth Circuit, which covers Kansas, Colorado, New Mexico, Oklahoma, Utah, and Wyoming, saw a 59 percent increase in farm bankruptcies over the same period. No wonder, as farm exports to China dropped to $9.1 billion from $19.5 billion in 2017—and kept falling in 2019. Meanwhile Canada's shipments of wheat to China increased more than 400 percent between 2017 and 2019.

Equilibrium extends to all. When farmers suffered, so did neighboring clothing stores and restaurants, grocery stores, and dry cleaners. By August 2019, bankruptcies in the Midwest were up 13 percent over 2018.

Big-picture, what had been a fairly stable equilibrium was now in transition. When the United States is seen as an unreliable trading partner, the rest of the world will pick up the slack, just as Vietnam, for example, acquired much of the business diverted from China due to the U.S. tariffs. If and when the United States returns to its status as a free-trade partner, the rest of the world will have already adjusted their trade patterns. It won't be so easy to rebuild those routes and relationships to what they once were, or to regain the dominance the United States once owned. When Detroit was building cars with short life expectancies, Japanese manufacturers stole market share with inexpensive, reliable cars. When Detroit started making better cars, they didn't get their market share back. Disruptions have consequences.

Trade is fundamental to the economic process. We aren't capable of being self-sufficient. Those who have tried have always been worse off for it. Others are better at some things than we are. So given our different capabilities, it is advantageous to trade with one another. You're not going to grow bananas in your backyard when you can go to a store and trade five minutes of your time, in terms of earnings, for a pound of bananas. You're better off and so are Hondurans. Free trade benefits both parties or they won't engage in it. Part of the value of trade is that it allows us to *not* do things we're not good at. Costa Rica is good at growing and exporting tropical fruits, but not at making cars, so they send pineapples to the United States and use the money to buy cars made in the United States.

America Can Profit from Its Advantage

As Alan Greenspan noted, "GDP is getting lighter." High value-added things used to weigh a lot; now the high-value-add is intellectual property, which can be shared around the world at very little expense.

The gains from that are enormous. Consider the film industry. A Hollywood movie might generate spectacular box office proceeds its opening weekend in the United States, but the take in China will be two or three times that and the numbers around the world bigger still. *Warcraft*, a 2016 film that cost $160 million to make, grossed less than $50 million in the United States but almost $400 million elsewhere.

The United States owns an advantage in this technological future and can continue to lead. That's preferable to trying to revert to what used to be, to restore jobs that are being done elsewhere more efficiently.

Emerging nations will eventually catch up to where the United States is today, but America can profit from its advantage now and continue advancing to remain relevant to itself as well as the rest of the world. Equilibrium will tell us where we stand.

The United States accounts for just 5 percent of the world's consumers, slightly less than Europe; more than 80 percent live in emerging nations, parts of the world looking to adopt work and consumption patterns that look like those in the United States. The United States is in position to exploit that lead.

In 1776, Adam Smith taught us how to become better off: let markets guide our decisions, not politics.

Takeaways

- Both parties are better off when they enter freely into a trade. If they aren't, the trade doesn't happen.
- International trade allows a much broader range of opportunities where different countries can benefit from their differing strengths.
- Innovations in transportation and logistics have facilitated trade.
- Today's supply chains are global in nature, and that global interdependence is essential to our economic well-being.

Equilibrium

Equilibrium is key to understanding the process and outcomes related to international trade. Any voluntary trade makes both parties to the trade better off; if one side thinks it isn't getting a desirable outcome, it won't complete the trade. The concept explains pretty much all commerce. We trade, usually money, for a good or service because we would rather have that good or service than the money it costs. It is a principle taken for granted when trade is local. But when trade crosses international boundaries, it is often seen in a different light, though it probably shouldn't be. Adam Smith, in The *Wealth of Nations*, was an early proponent of the idea that free trade between countries makes both countries better off. Tariffs and other restrictions on trade may make some segments of a domestic economy better off by being protected from foreign competition, but that protection comes at the cost of higher consumer prices, and with the higher prices, less consumption.

CHAPTER 17

The Compensation Principle: Should We Pay the Losers?

Whenever changes are made in economic policy, there are almost always winners and losers. How should we balance those interests?

When we impose tariffs on foreign producers, we help domestic producers of the same goods by allowing them to charge more. That's a win for those producers. But everyone who buys the product domestically will pay the higher price; they're the losers in the deal. In general we're better off engaging in free trade, but whether society is better off for protecting U.S. manufacturers and workers' jobs than allowing for more competitive pricing is difficult to judge. Gains from tariffs are typically shared by a few producers; the losses, while small case by case, are spread among all consumers and in total usually outweigh the gains. But the gains are concentrated and the losses diffuse, and the few and big beneficiaries can pressure policymakers and influence political action. The dichotomy is an integral part of almost every economic policy decision; there are few cases where all policymakers' constituents are better off and no one is worse off.

Understanding and accepting that a change in economic policy creates losers as well as winners, the challenge is determining if the losses are worth the gains. Most changes are not so clear-cut that you can determine the balance before enacting the change. The ideal that policy decisions will be made for the greater good of the greater number of people is not so easily achieved. Or consider a decision that makes many people better by making a few much worse off. For example, limiting social safety nets might provide tax relief for most but leave some homeless or starving.

While economists like to talk about individuals maximizing their utility, they can't calculate interpersonal comparisons of well-being. We can say one person likes chocolate ice cream and another vanilla, but not by how much in a way that allows us to sum up the difference. Policymaking would be easier if you could quantify the comparison, and many ways have been proposed to determine how to make choices that will make society better off, but no one formula has been landed on—and there is substantial theoretical reasoning to believe that a grand "social welfare function" can't be built.

Winners and Losers

Still, decisions must be made. The compensation principle suggests that a policy change may be acceptable if the winners will be so much better off that you could take something from them to restore the losers to at least as well off as they were prior to the new policy. If the winners compensate the losers appropriately and still have gains, there is, in principle, a net social benefit. In practice, there can be administrative challenges, but there are plenty of examples of the principle at work. When the United States, Canada, and Mexico opened up trade under the North American Free Trade Agreement (NAFTA) in 1994, the idea was that North American society would be better off net-net with a free trade zone. To compensate the losers, primarily U.S. manufacturing workers who lost their jobs, the United States invested tax revenue in federal retraining programs. Whether that was sufficient is arguable, but the jobs programs were aimed at making the losers to the trade agreement better off than without compensation. In that case the losers didn't directly draw resources from the companies that were winners but society paid with tax revenues.

The compensation principle is not an all-purpose decision-making tool; it is not a way to make judgment calls. And often compensation doesn't happen. The decision might be based on making society better, but redistributing the gains so the losers are at least as well off as before is an enormous problem. Chalk it up to time-inconsistent preferences. At all levels of policymaking, any meaningful policy change will have winners and losers. We can impose all kinds of criteria and requirements on the option we adopt, but many of those decisions assume compensation that in practice doesn't happen.

Perhaps the most attractive attribute of the compensation principle is that it makes the case that if the winners can't compensate the losers, if the gains to the winners are less than the losses to the losers, you shouldn't implement the policy. It says there has to be a net gain to society that, at least in principle, can be distributed to make everyone as well off as they were before the policy change, including as it relates to such issues as income immobility and inequality.

Pareto Outcomes

The compensation principle's roots are in the earliest of economic thought, as a means for determining what will make a society better. It was a key step in the progression of economic thinking in terms of social decision-making, codified around the turn of the nineteenth century by Vilfredo Pareto, an Italian engineer and economist, who used the concept in his studies of economic efficiency and income distribution. Pareto said you ought to make decisions based on the criteria of whether people are better or worse off after a change.

We still refer to a change that makes everyone better off as a Pareto superior outcome. Eliminating an antiquated regulatory burden, something you have to comply with but technology has made obsolete, is a Pareto superior outcome. If you're planning a birthday party and everyone wants chocolate ice cream, and you get it instead of the planned mix of flavors, that's Pareto superior. A Pareto optimal outcome occurs when we reach a state where no one's condition can be improved without making someone else's condition worse off as a result of a decision. The compensation principle is an attempt at a practical application of Pareto optimality.

Pareto optimality is useful in answering many questions about policymaking. The concept is particularly useful in framing a common dilemma facing policymakers when no one can be made better off by a particular policy decision without making someone else worse off.

The compensation principle is about making social choices, but often doesn't provide guidance when dealing with particularly thorny questions because the gains and losses are difficult to compare. In most cases, the ambiguities of making decisions can't be answered. Consider the difference in political parties, which is most fundamentally a difference in philosophies, disagreement over what values are best for society.

Takeaways

- Whenever there is a change in economic policy, there will be winners and losers. The challenge is determining if the losses are worth the gains.
- The compensation principle suggests that in making a change where the winners will be so much better off, you take something from the winners to restore the losers to at least as well off as they were prior to the new economic policy.
- A change that makes everyone better off is known by economists as a Pareto superior outcome.
- A Pareto optimal outcome refers to a state where no one can be made better off without making someone else worse off.
- In most cases the ambiguities of making decisions can't be answered by either of these approaches.

Equilibrium

Helping societies decide among different policy options is a major economic challenge. We know that free trade can make an economy better off, but there will be some losers in the process. Unfortunately, the gains from trade, while potentially large, tend to be diffuse, while the losers from trade tend to be concentrated. The compensation principle suggests that if, after the policy change, the winners can compensate the losers for the losses, then the change is probably appropriate. The problem, of course, is that compensation rarely actually happens. Still, it is part of the motive behind federal programs that provide aid to industries and workers that have been displaced by foreign competition. Decisions like this tend to be complex because, as Pareto observed, we are usually in a state of equilibrium where there is no change that can make someone better off without making someone else worse off.

CHAPTER 18

Domestic Imbalance: A Role for Trade Balances

Almost always trade involves the exchange of goods or services for money. The seller wants money, and key to the execution of the trade, the buyer wants the product or service and has the money. When it's domestic, we consider the process balanced. There's usually an increase in GDP as a result, if an unremarkable one. It's trade and it's how commerce happens.

But when it's across borders, we talk about trade differently. When a seller from abroad sends goods or services into the U.S. economy in exchange for money, we call it an unbalanced trade or a trade deficit. We see goods or services being imported but no domestically produced equivalent exported. It's goods exchanged for money or some other form of financial asset. And when we trade financial assets of whatever sort for goods or services, it adds to our trade deficit.

It's important to recognize that in all cases the trade really is balanced. It's just that the flow of goods and services is viewed differently from the flow of assets. And it matters. If a foreign nation accumulates a great deal of U.S. financial assets they can claim some share of the current output of our economy. They can buy hard assets or import goods into their country using our assets. That's a long-run concern associated with trade deficits. Short term, they might dislocate U.S. employment because the goods are produced abroad rather than domestically. In the longer run by allowing the foreign nation to accumulate financial claims, the United States could become a net debtor to that country.

Of course, simply buying goods from abroad is not in itself worrisome. After all, a trade doesn't happen unless both parties think they will be better off by making it. It is a principal reason to buy a product from abroad: our trading partner does a better job making it than we do. We buy bananas from Costa Rica because they produce a better banana.

Another way of thinking about trade imbalances is at the macroeconomic level. When our domestic economy is trying to consume more than it is producing, it can only achieve that by importing the difference. The imbalance in production and consumption needs to be made up by goods from abroad, which we can do by issuing financial assets to our trading partners, essentially IOUs in exchange for goods and services. If we are exporting goods in exchange for the imported goods, then we haven't made any headway in our desire to consume more than we produce. It is the same as an individual consumer spending more than their income by taking on debt.

Of course, our trading partner has to want to take our financial assets. A country with persistent deficits and imbalances faces the possibility of a debt crisis, where the rest of the world doesn't want any more financial assets, no more debt, from that country. Like the individual consumer to whom no one is willing to extend credit can spend only what they make.

The Monetary Approach to the Balance of Payments

In the 1960s, economist Robert Mundell proposed what he called the "monetary approach to the balance of payments" as an explanation of why some countries have persistent trade deficits. His idea was that if an economy had a surplus of money—the central bank or government issued more financial assets than the domestic economy wanted—the economy would shed the excess in exchange for foreign goods and services. Mundell saw the excess supply of financial assets as a money market imbalance that was driving trade deficits. Equilibrium in the financial assets market would be restored by exporting the excess in exchange for real, not financial, foreign assets.

It is useful to think about this in personal terms. When we go to the supermarket to buy food, we intend to give up financial assets in exchange for food. If we buy food, we have a trade deficit with the supermarket. We may worry about that deficit if our need for food continuously exceeds our supply of additional money to pay for it. But it is not clear what drove the deficit with the supermarket. Was it the supermarket that enticed us to part with our assets, or was it us who, having the money, wanted to buy food? In reality it is both. The supermarket wants us to part with our money in exchange for food and we want the food and are willing to part with our money to get it.

If we focus solely on the flow of goods, we have a misleading view of the trade process. Mundell's insight was to emphasize the flow going in the opposite direction: the willingness of an economy to give up financial assets in exchange for goods and services. He reversed the traditional approach to trade imbalances of looking at the markets for goods and services to looking at the financial markets that were supporting the purchasing of the good or service.

Mundell's theory, emphasizing the joint relationship between the flow of goods in one direction and the flow of assets in the other, was a step toward what is known as the twin-deficits argument, which suggests that an increase in the federal deficit will have an adverse impact on our trade deficit. When our government decides to increase its deficit, it issues additional debt. The debt must be held somewhere, and foreign economies may want it because they find our government debt attractive. The rest of the world then has to provide goods and services in order to purchase that debt. So one way of looking at the state of the U.S. international trade balance is that financing requirements for the U.S. federal deficit combined with the attractiveness of U.S. financial assets means that an increase in the federal deficit will be in some way matched by an increase in the trade deficit. That is, if the United States offers to increase government debt and some nation outside the United States wants to hold our debt, it will have to sell goods or services into the United States to acquire that debt. The outflow of the debt is matched by an inflow of goods. But it is the desire of the foreign entity to own U.S. debt, not only U.S. consumers' desire to buy the foreign goods that drives the trade imbalance. That chain of causation is the reverse of how we often hear trade deficits described.

Empirically, when we look at the long-term relationship between trade and fiscal deficits in the United States post–World War II, it wasn't until the 1970s that we began running both systematic trade deficits and systematic fiscal deficits. The match-up is not perfect but close enough to be of concern. In more formal terms, the empirical evidence of twin-deficit mutuality has been mixed, but still strong enough to keep the idea around as an important component in thinking about trade imbalances.

In a grand sense, the United States is responsible for its own trade deficits and international debt. But more subtly, it involves more than just sending jobs to China, India, Viet Nam, or Mexico. It's also the case that our financial assets are in demand by the rest of the world, which is why they're willing to give us bananas or cars for our IOUs. In this way of thinking trade deficits may be somewhat benign, and maybe even a good deal. If the rest of the world is eager to buy U.S. debt, maybe the United States should take advantage of that. But only up to a point that time-inconsistent preference may again pose a problem. Those IOUs represent claims on assets of the United States that could be redeemed, demanded to be satisfied, at sometime in the future, even if currently the world is willing to hold U.S. debt—as long as the United States does not let itself get overextended. Like the individual that has a good credit rating in part because they haven't borrowed too much money.

If we take an equilibrium view of trade deficits, it's fair to say the rest of the world plays a role in the U.S. deficit. As emerging economies grow, they build up savings, and it makes sense for those economies to diversify their financial portfolio, which means it makes sense to have a portion of their savings in the form of U.S. debt, as it is relatively safe. To the extent countries want U.S. Treasury securities in their portfolios, the rest of the world is contributing to our trade deficit. As we see the amount of savings around the world increase, and some of those offshore savings make their way into Treasuries, that's going to add to our trade deficit.

A Broader View of Trade

From one perspective, much of the hand wringing over our trade deficit emanates from how we define it. Trade is always balanced in the sense that two parties willingly agree to execute a trade, and if either side believes they will be worse off as a result of the trade, it won't occur. What makes the trade "unbalanced" is that the two parties sit in different countries. Still, the broader, long-term result of unbalanced goods and services trading is something we need to pay attention to as the world accumulates our financial assets. In the short run, things are more complicated than losing U.S. jobs abroad; it includes sending U.S. dollars abroad and the eagerness of the rest of the world to take those financial assets that makes the deficit possible.

In the United States, if I offer you a dollar for a good or service, you have to take the U.S. currency. But rest of the world takes it not because they have to but because they want to. We want the goods more than the money, and they want the money more than the goods. What happens when trading partners no longer want to take debt, currency or other financial assets, for goods from a country but want something tangible in exchange for their existing accumulation of financial assets? If it all happens gradually, it's likely not a problem, but if it happens all at once it's a debt crisis and it cripples a country's economy, trashes the value of its currency, and renders it economically undesirable.

As long as the United States maintains its standing as a safe financial harbor, our trading partners are not likely to call our debt. And the demand for a safe-harbor long-term asset globally is increasing. For now, as opposed to calling our debt, our trading partners want more U.S. Treasuries.

Takeaways

- When a seller from abroad sends goods or services into the U.S. economy in exchange for U.S. money, we call it an "unbalanced trade."
- If a foreign nation accumulates a lot of U.S. financial assets they have claims to the current output of our economy. If they choose to redeem those assets in a short period of time, it may be disruptive to our domestic economy.
- An imbalance in production and consumption needs to be made up by goods from abroad, which a nation can do, contributing to its trade deficit by issuing financial assets to its trading partners, essentially IOUs in exchange for goods and services.
- Robert Mundell extended existing thinking about deficits in the 1960s with his monetary approach to the balance of payments theory, which proposes that instead of looking at

imbalances in the goods markets as an explanation for trade deficits, it may be a money market imbalance, an excess supply of financial assets, driving trade deficits.

- The rest of the world is contributing to the U.S. trade deficit by wanting to hold relatively safe U.S. securities in their portfolios. This isn't usually a bad thing; we want our debt to be readily accepted or even sought after worldwide.
- The concern over the U.S. trade deficit is about the amount of debt to foreign nations and whether the United States could meet the demand if they called the debt.

Equilibrium

In a general equilibrium, both parties in a trade feel they are better off as a consequence of the deal, whether the United States is buying bananas from Central America or Central America is willing to part with their bananas for U.S. financial assets. The flow of goods and services in one direction must be matched by the flow of financial claims in the other direction. The goods and financial markets must simultaneously accommodate each other, and figuring out whether it is the U.S. demand for foreign goods, or the foreign demand for U.S. financial assets that is driving the trade imbalance is tricky.

CHAPTER 19

As the World Turns

The United States makes up about 4 percent of the world's consumers; the 19 states of the Euro area only slightly more. More than 80 percent of the world's population lives in what economists classify as emerging economies. Of course, some emerging economies are more advanced than others. But outside of North America, Europe, Japan, and Australia, more or less everybody else is emerging—a very large pool of potential consumers whose income is growing.

Perhaps the most fundamental, and obvious, of all economic principles is that if you're selling something, you're better off if that thing is something people want to buy. It is relevant in a discussion of the character of trade with emerging economies because the incomes of people in emerging economies are increasing more rapidly than the incomes of people in industrialized, or developed, nations.

Advantages of Proven Technologies

Emerging economies are catching up to leading industrial economies, on one hand, because they don't have to invest in developing cutting edge technology, only in the best of the already proven technologies. They might not deliver the benefits of a superior technology, but neither did the emerging economy have to absorb the costs of developing technologies that didn't work out. So an emerging economy gets a huge gain in income from implementing a relatively unsophisticated production process that is proven, and that can be implemented inexpensively and quickly because it is proven.

Just a few decades ago, China was making furniture for export with hand drills. Moving to digitally controlled processes led to huge productivity enhancements, spectacular gains in productivity. Those processes had been in place for many years in the United States and other industrialized

nations' furniture factories. Total factor productivity, the combined productivity of capital and labor, while noisy for both the United States and
China, has been notably greater in China since 1980 (See figure 19.1).

Agriculture is another industry in emerging countries ripe for increases
in productivity. Switching from plows and animals to tractors, even the
most unsophisticated tractors, allows a farm community to plow more
land faster with far less labor. The established technology is relatively
easy to adopt because it's understood and inexpensive and can deliver
exponential growth in productivity.

Telecommunications historically has been a major challenge for unde-
veloped nations. But wireless technology is providing a solution. Emerging economies have been able to skip the expense and logistical challenges
associated with installing landline communications by building cell tow-
ers. They might not have 5G connectivity but they do have smartphones

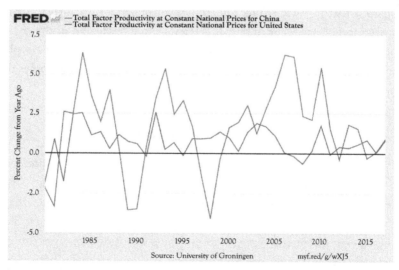

**Figure 19.1 Swings in total factor productivity: China and the
United States**

Source: U.S. Census Bureau

Source: U.S. Department of Housing and Urban Development. Release: New Residential Sales
Units: Thousands, Seasonally Adjusted Annual Rate

Frequency: Monthly U.S. Census Bureau and U.S. Department of Housing and Urban Development, New One Family Houses Sold: United States [HSN1F], retrieved from FRED,

Federal Reserve Bank of St. Louis; https://fred.stlouisfed.org/series/HSN1F,
October 26, 2020.

that do far more than allow people to talk to each other and have made enormous strides in providing communications technology that is not very expensive.

More Money, Better Things

Implementing developed technologies and processes is helping a large segment of the globe grow incomes more rapidly in terms of buying power than industrialized nations where growth is constrained by the capital investment required to research, develop, and produce new advances.

With greater incomes, people in emerging economies buy more goods and services, and not only more of the same goods and services they bought before. They can buy better things. We see that first in emerging economies in improved diets and healthier lifestyles, evidenced, at least in part, in taller people. Anecdotally, higher income is also moving emerging peoples from the ravages of limited food to the first-world problem of being able to afford a worse diet, consuming foods we're better off not consuming.

Increased consumption doesn't stop with food. From bikes to motorcycles to cars, emerging nations are moving up the consumption chain across the board to higher value products. Many of those products are manufactured in the United States as the United States has moved toward making high-value products.

The United States largely gave up making low value-added products in the latter half of the twentieth century. Processes and plants for cut-and-sew operations, low value-added manufacturing, and labor-intensive manufacturing moved offshore. The exodus was painful for many parts of the United States, in particular the South which lost the majority of its apparel manufacturing industry just as the Northeast United States had when textile manufacturers moved their operations to Southern locations a century earlier. Today the abandoned textile mills in Georgia are reminiscent of the same scenes 150 years ago in the Northeast.

The United States is relatively good at making the high-value products the emerging world is shifting their buying toward as their incomes rise. The secular trend favors exports of things made in the United States. Other countries will try to emulate the United States, knock-off our products and technologies, but we have a considerable lead in expertise, infrastructure, and investment in making high value-added products. And it is not so easy to knock off very high value-add products. Gulfstream and Lear have international competitors in the corporate jet space but are extremely successful and recognized as high-end brands. Many U.S.-made highly engineered medical devices are in great demand around the world.

Services as Exports

High net worth people around the world with health issues come to name brand hospitals in the U.S. for treatment. The United States has also been a major exporter of education. A degree from a top U.S. university is held in high esteem internationally.

Health care, education, and the like are intangible exports. We have benefited dramatically from investing and innovating in these areas, and can continue to do so. There has been some hesitation to consider—and difficulty in measuring—such intangible services as exports, but their value to the U.S. economy is enormous. The out-of-country tuitions foreign students pay to U.S. universities and graduate schools make up a notable portion of our export economy and a substantial credit to the balance of trade, not to mention the universities' cash flows. Tourism is also contributing an increasing share of the overall portion of the balance of trade provided by high value-added exported services. And the economic benefits are spread throughout the country—at least they were pre-COVID-19.

Exported services won't turn around the trade deficit in the short term, but they will increasingly make their impact long term. COVID slowed that trend but did not make it any less important to pay attention to service exports. It's easier to calculate the merchandise side of our exports, how U.S.-branded goods sell abroad. But it's also easy to recognize the value of U.S. service exports. Just look around the world to count the number of highly placed public and private sector officials and office holders with U.S. degrees.

Takeaways

- More than 80 percent of the world's population lives in what economists classify as emerging economies, a large and growing market.
- The incomes of people in emerging economies are increasing more rapidly than incomes of people in industrialized, or developed, nations.
- Emerging economies are catching up to leading industrial economies, to a large extent because they don't have to invest in developing cutting edge technology, only in already proven technologies.
- With greater incomes, people in emerging economies buy not only more, but better goods and services, those with a higher value-add. It is first seen in improved diets, but spreads across the entire consumption bundle.
- The United States is relatively good at making the high-value products the emerging world is shifting toward as their incomes rise.
- The United States leads the world in exports of health care and education.
- Exported services won't turn around the trade deficit in the short term, but they will increasingly make an impact in the long term.

Equilibrium

Emerging economies are gaining in income and changing what they consume toward a bundle closer to what industrial economies consume. It spells an emerging and very large market for the goods and services the United States is already producing, and includes high value-added services such as education. This secular trend is not fast moving, but it can make a substantial contribution over time if the United States acts to take advantage of the evolving global economy.

PART III

The Economy and You

CHAPTER 20

COVID-19: How the Pandemic Changed Business

This time it was different.

Typically recessions happen when consumption slows due to a perceived imbalance or problematic issue in the economy. People fear a decline in their income long term and stop buying things they deem unnecessary, which slows the economy, which leads to layoffs, which takes the nation into a recession. But that wasn't the case in 2020. The economy looked strong and sustainable. We were near full employment; many companies and industries were having trouble getting appropriately skilled workers. Then came COVID-19. In the middle of March the U.S. economy essentially shut down. More than 20 million people lost their jobs in the month of April (compared to 800,000 during the worst month of the Great Recession). Never had the United States experienced employment losses anywhere near this scale.

The causes of a recession, or the events that lead to a recession, are usually internal: the overinvestment by some of the world's largest financial institutions in haphazardly valued financial instruments backed by questionably valued real estate that led to the 2008 recession, the dot-com bubble that led to a recession in 2001, the 1929 stock market crash that gave way to the Great Depression. But this time it was an external force, a virus that worked to close down most of the economy.

Had the virus been controlled, had it disappeared shortly after it appeared, the role for policy makers would have been relatively small. People had both the means and the motive to continue with their lives as they were. Fundamentally the economy was in good shape; COVID-19 would have been an economic hiccup. Surely the impact on some would have been serious, but for most the disruption would have been short term. But it didn't end early and challenged policy makers like they had never been challenged.

A Cataclysmic Business Decline

COVID-19 was a natural disaster. But unlike most natural disasters it was not limited to a small geographic area; it was global in scope. For a natural disaster, like a hurricane of flood, policy makers can provide bridge loans for otherwise well-functioning businesses for a few months while the area gets rebuilt. Extending loans to otherwise viable businesses to bridge the period of dislocation caused by the natural disaster is a reasonable strategy. This time, however, we didn't know how long the bridge needed to be. Early on, policy makers established stimulus and bridge loan programs, but they were unable to determine how long they would be applied and structured them to cover only a few months. Until some sense that the pandemic was under control, it was difficult to know what to do to keep some form of relief going. We didn't need the pandemic to end, only to see a light at the end of the tunnel to determine how substantial these transitory support measures needed to be and how long they needed to be in place.

It was a public health problem, not so much an economic problem. But the longer it persisted the more severe the economic issues. A very short period without income has a different impact than a longer-term loss where the consequences build over time. Businesses faced uncertain times to reopening, and uncertainty was costly as they made provisional spending decisions that too often proved dead wrong. The shock to the global economy was unprecedented, three times worse than the 2008 financial crisis according to a September 2020 report by the World Economic Forum (www.weforum.org/agenda/2020/09/an-economist-explains-what-covid-19-has-done-to-the-global-economy/).

On the heels of a resurgence across Europe in early fall, a second wave of COVID-19 swept through the United States, more than a million new cases in each of two weeks in mid-November. It was obvious that economies globally were struggling or stalled until an effective treatment or a vaccine was in place.

Winners and Losers

In many ways the pandemic only accelerated changes in our economy that were already taking place. At a 2005 national conference of bankers, one of the questions in an attendee survey asked respondents what they would like to see technology do for workers in the future. At least one person from every bank represented at the conference responded that they wanted to do their job from the beach. No other question or issue was answered with such uniformity.

Nor was the sentiment limited to the banking industry. We had believed for some time that it wasn't going to be necessary to be in an office building to conduct many forms of commerce. But our hand was forced in March 2020 to test that feasibility on a national scale. Some estimates had more than 30 percent of the workforce working outside their usual workplace environment through the spring and summer. Many worked at home not only because it was viable, but because it was the default option. What American calling to schedule a plumber or air conditioning service didn't hear a barking dog or crying child in the background? For that matter, how many Zoom meetings featured interrupting children or pets in the background—or foreground?

For most workers, staying home is not feasible—manufacturing workers of course, retail and restaurant workers, and logistics and transit workers. You can't drive a truck from your living room. But a large portion of the workforce at all skill levels can work from home, from simple data entry work to sophisticated professional services like telemedicine and accounting. It is clear that businesses have not only learned to cope with not having everyone show up at nine o'clock on Monday mornings at the same location, but are finding efficiencies in letting employees work remotely. The world is unlikely to return to life as it was.

Logistics was clearly a winner among COVID-19 survivors. The continued growth of online shopping and the associated distribution has required a much larger logistics workforce. Logistics also benefited from the disruptions to supply chains, which led many firms to rethink how their products and materials for making products are delivered and has created a huge surge in warehousing and warehouse construction.

Many of the losers were small businesses and their employees, like restaurants and theaters and other entertainment venues that in many cases had to shut down or dramatically cut back the number of people they could serve at any one sitting. Many small businesses simply didn't have the financial wherewithal to survive once the relief funds stopped coming. But many of the losers were businesses already under pressure, where trends counter to the way they operated were already in play and simply rushed by the virus. Small retailers without substantial online presences and sales or a particularly strong niche were among the first and most numerous to go. Malls, including regional and superregional malls and their owner-operators, already losing shoppers to online retailers, had been trying to reinvent themselves as entertainment venues with restaurants and theaters. As more landlords struggled, their lenders faced difficult decisions, to lower and sometimes forgive rents or restructure mortgage loans, or foreclose on a property, sometimes a property with no apparent alternative use. That will continue to play out over the coming years, and properties that decline in value will have to take a valuation hit; losses will be recognized.

Commercial and Residential Real Estate

The pandemic threw the commercial real estate market into a spin as offices emptied to the extent they could and virtual collaboration became the norm. Much of the workforce that proved they could be productive working from home—or the beach—did not return to full-time office occupation. Businesses began reconfiguring not only their spaces but their plans about how to use space, and where they want their office locations, including a departure from prestigious urban high-rises.

Consider the logistical challenges associated with a meeting for a hundred people on the 50th floor of a high-rise in light of the need for physical distancing in elevators. It would take hours to get everyone up to the meeting and hours again to get them back down. Companies learned that virtual meetings work quite well, in particular for large groups that involve presentations and interaction that can be accommodated online. And they save attendees the time and cost of travel and the disruption in their lives. You might lose some benefits of networking, but the efficiencies outweigh the losses on a cost–benefit basis.

Prior to the pandemic, single-family housing construction was not keeping pace with the growth in U.S. population. Gen Xers and millennials gravitated initially to multifamily housing and were staying longer than previous generations. But the pandemic moved them toward the more private life of single-family homes. Residential housing sales exploded. Again much of the movement was going to happen, but the pandemic gave people thinking of moving out of multifamily buildings a reason to do it sooner than later (See Figure 20.1).

As well, a large number of low-income workers in industries like leisure and travel lost their jobs and their ability to pay rent. As the pandemic raged on, the world was looking at an impending and sweeping

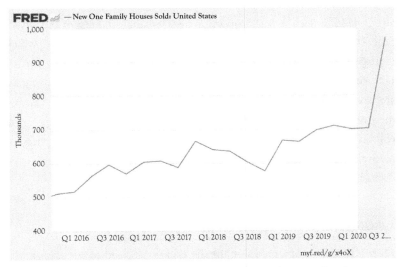

Figure 20.1 *The pandemic generated a new preference for the privacy associated with single-family housing*

Source: U.S. Census Bureau

Source: U.S. Department of Housing and Urban Development

Release: New Residential Sales

Units: Thousands, Seasonally Adjusted Annual Rate

Frequency: Monthly

U.S. Census Bureau and U.S. Department of Housing and Urban Development,

New One Family Houses Sold: United States [HSN1F],

retrieved from FRED,

Federal Reserve Bank of St. Louis;

https://fred.stlouisfed.org/series/HSN1F,

October 26, 2020.

eviction crisis. One disquieting trend was that as people addressed their own crises by downsizing to smaller, less expensive apartments, it was easier for low-income property managers to evict those unable to make timely rent payments in favor of others looking to move in. Those low-income renters were more likely to be renting from relatively unsophisticated owners and investors than large, professionally managed complexes, and the challenges faced by the landlords as well as the tenants extended to the mortgage holders. As late as November, various studies, including one by The Aspen Institute, were estimating that as many as forty million tenants were at risk of eviction by the end of 2020 (www.aspeninstitute. org/blog-posts/the-covid-19-eviction-crisis-an-estimated-30-40-million-people-in-america-are-at-risk/).

While consumption decreased globally during the pandemic and after, the U.S. decline was proportionately less than the rest of the world. Still, the rest of the world bought less from the United States, which increased the trade deficit, and in a deeper sense sent a warning for the U.S. economy. When our trading partners, who buy as well as supply us, are shutdown, we have a difficult time restoring our economy because there are far fewer consumers we can sell our goods and services to. There will be less demand for our surplus of natural gas, agricultural exports, or corporate jets; foreign citizens won't travel to the United States for leisure or business, for education or health care.

Takeaways

- The causes of a recession, or the events that lead to a recession, are usually internal, but for the COVID-19 recession it was an external force, a virus that worked to close down most of the economy.
- COVID-19 was a natural disaster. But unlike most natural disasters, it was not limited to a small geographic area but global in scope.
- Logistics was a winner among COVID-19 survivors. The ongoing growth of online shopping and the associated distribution has required a much larger logistics workforce and created a huge surge in warehousing and warehouse construction.

- Many of the losers were businesses already under pressure, where trends counter to the way they operated were already in play and simply rushed by the virus.
- Residential housing exploded from a quarter of a million single-family homes in 2019 to four million on an annualized basis through the first three quarters of 2020.
- When our trading partners, who buy as well as supply us, are shut down, we have a difficult time restoring our economy because there are fewer consumers outside the United States to sell our goods and services to.

Equilibrium

Equilibrium in the economy is a dynamic process that was severely disrupted by the COVID-19 pandemic. The short-term illnesses, deaths, and job losses were unprecedented in our lifetimes. Nonetheless, the fundamentals underlying the economy remained intact. The decline in incomes and consumption worked together to cause the misery of a recession. The global nature of the shock made full recovery a much longer and more challenging process. And the pandemic forced our hand, so to speak, in speeding up many longer-term trends, for better or worse.

CHAPTER 21

Climate Change: "Is It Hot in Here or Is It Me?" (Joan of Arc)

We'll leave the argument over the cause or causes of climate change, the discussion of the science of climate change, and even environmental economics to the specialists who write voluminously about those subjects. However, we can address some of the implications of the impact of climate on the U.S. and global economies.

What economics does for science is provide a motive for accumulating data. Lloyds of London has data on hurricanes dating back centuries, not so much due to an interest in hurricane science but because they were insuring ships. They needed to track storms that threatened vessels so they could determine risk and premiums. As such, that discipline, a facet of environmental economics, preceded what we call economics today, and originally, political economics. Climate has an enormous impact on commerce, and those mounds of related data gathered over decades and centuries are, in a way, accidentally of great use in understanding how our climate is changing.

Climate and commerce are historically and inevitably interconnected in how they influence physical economic development. In those initial centuries Lloyds was insuring ships, commerce was based essentially on moving things by boat, if some movement was by land along the Silk Road. By and large trade was done in ports, and fostered the development of the largest cities. Even in the United States, there are few large landlocked cities, and those—Atlanta, Dallas, Denver, Phoenix—became large relatively recently.

With the advent of climate change, port cities began facing disproportionate challenges. If the kind of tropical storm that flooded New
York City's subways in 2019 had been a recurring incident over years, the
subways would have been designed and built differently, that is, to withstand floods. There are posh neighborhoods in Miami where the streets
routinely flood during a high tide and full moon. Such persistent events
call into question the ongoing viability of some of these locations—and
present a major challenge to our economy.

Evaluations and Insurance

Climate change threatens property valuations. Homes on beachfronts that
are not elevated to withstand today's storm surges are subject to devalu-
ation. Property valuations are forward-looking, and within a decade or
so these homes may be considered uninsurable, unviable, perhaps even
unusable.

Insurance is not just about compensating for contemporaneous damages, but assessing the probability of those damages over time—for example, flood insurance for a mountain cabin versus a cottage on a barrier
island. Premiums are "experience rated," but those years of experience
are not as useful as in the past for establishing risks today. Homebuyers
in California know that the Santa Ana winds come every fall when the
state is dry and at risk of fires. But now those fires are widespread, all up
and down the West Coast, well beyond the areas traditionally subject to
the Santa Ana winds, even into Colorado and the Rockies. Fire insurance
valuations based on historic experience substantially underestimate the
current risks. The implications extend to the entire economy because risks
are shared. If you live in that mountain cabin and your risk of fire is essentially unchanged over the last decade, you might be in an insurance pool
with greater exposure and the associated higher premiums.

Insurance companies may make good faith efforts to provide insurance at fair prices, but climate change has made it difficult if not impossible to determine actuarially fair pricing. That translates to greater
uncertainties and disruptions of property valuations. Climate change
makes it difficult to value and difficult to assess risks, which makes it
difficult to insure, and insurance is a part of the valuation process. It is a
big and unpleasant loop.

Carbon Taxing

Climate change affects property values and how they are assessed, in part because of property rights and how the actions of some impact the properties of others. We have yet to perfect a way to assess the value of the pollution from vehicles and manufacturing plants in terms of the larger setting of global climate change. It might be possible to do so theoretically but not in a practical sense. Our approach has been to assign the responsibility broadly by regulating vehicles or industries that pollute.

Economists favor a carbon tax because it addresses the overuse of one particular input creating an environmental problem. If carbon-based emissions cause environmental damage, then taxing the use of carbon is a direct way of discouraging carbon-based pollution. A carbon tax has not been politically popular in the United States; a large portion of our energy depends on carbon and a carbon tax would result in a tax increase for a large swath of our population. It would also make for dramatic changes in how we power vehicles. Vehicles that emit a great deal of carbon exhaust would be economically disadvantaged, as would carbon-intensive industries.

The negative externalities associated with pollution and property rights are massive and global in nature. While the United States might make strides in curbing pollution, we are a large emitter because we are a large economy. One of the top concerns of environmental economists is that other nations trying to become large might not have the same level of commitment to the environment as the United States and other developed nations.

Takeaways

- It is fundamentally more difficult today to value large segments of the physical structure of U.S. cities that are located near bodies of water or in the West, and enormous risks from rising seas and fires make them increasingly difficult to insure.
- The combination of property valuations and insurance as affected by climate change disrupts financial markets, particularly property- and insurance-related markets.

- A carbon tax is popular with economists because it directly addresses the overuse of one particular input creating an environmental problem.

Equilibrium

Things interact with each other in ways that aren't always immediately obvious. Climate change, for example, casts uncertainty on the long-term viability, or at least valuation, of some currently very important properties because of the increased probability of some expensive natural disaster. Given the likelihood of increasingly frequent and damaging natural disasters, it is difficult to figure out risk-appropriate insurance rates. The uncertainty in insurance markets adds further uncertainty to valuing property where insurance is a critical part of the valuation. That simultaneous system of uncertainties in prices and values becomes increasingly problematic as climate change accelerates.

CHAPTER 22

Health Care Costs: A Steady Climb

The life expectancy of a U.S. citizen in 2020 was nearly 79 years, about 11 years longer than in 1950. The shorter life spans of past decades were at least partially due to behavior: adults smoked, ate more salty, sugary, greasy food, and weren't as exercise conscious as twenty-first century Americans. Many in their mid-sixties had heart attacks—and died. Today, we do much better, from about 600 deaths from heart disease per one hundred thousand Americans in 1950—700 per hundred thousand males—to fewer than 165 per hundred thousand in 2017 (www.cdc.gov/nchs/data/hus/2018/005.pdf). Heart disease remains the number one killer of Americans, but only about 2 percent of the 30 million people diagnosed with heart disease in 2019 perished. Generally we recover, even if it does cost us enormous sums of money in cardiac care.

We enjoy improved health in part because we live healthier lifestyles. But life has also been lengthened considerably by improvements in medical technology and services. The health care economy continues to grow, increasing in 2018 to about 17 percent of GDP. You're pleased to make that contribution, particularly if you are insured, because you would probably be less healthy if you didn't. But apart from its chunk of GDP, the cost of health care is concerning, particularly to the uninsured. In evaluating health care spending, we need to distinguish between simple inflation in health services—simply paying more for the same thing—and an improvement in what we are buying that costs more.

It's not easy to distinguish costs on a quality-adjusted basis. You're paying more for the treatment of your cardiac event but getting a bigger payoff by not dying. How much of that higher cardiac care bill is due to health care inflation and how much to a better quality product? Sorting that out is compounded by the common practice of cost-shifting, whereby hospitals charge different clients different prices for the same treatment based on whether or not they have insurance, or if they do, what their insurance companies have negotiated with the hospital or other health care provider.

Cost Versus Outcomes

The United States spends more per capita on health care than any other industrialized nation. But our health care metrics are not correspondingly superior. We don't lead the pack in outcomes; in fact, we lead only in spending. Part of that is the bifurcation of outcomes. If you are relatively well employed and well insured you enjoy some of best health care in the world and good outcomes. But for a large segment of the U.S. population, people who do not have high incomes and are not insured, the outcomes are not good. Among a multitude of evidence is the decline in average life expectancy among poorly educated white women, a turn never before seen in the United States. While widespread drug use in some communities contributes to the decline, it is more a function of the split in the ways health care is delivered. It is also a primary consideration in the debate over how we deal with health care going forward.

As health care costs continue to soar and cost containment becomes an increasingly pressing issue, much of the focus is on paying for treating the uninsured. Consider the micro-clinics that have sprung up in pharmacies. If you have health insurance and are marginally ill—a sore throat, a fever—you go to a micro-clinic or urgent care center and in a relatively short time and for relatively little money, typically a small insurance copay, you get a test for strep throat and a prescription for a drug to treat it and you go on with your life. It's an easy and cost-efficient way to address and cure your illness before it becomes a serious disease. But if you are uninsured and don't have the cash to pay for your visit, test, and drugs, you stay home, get sicker, and wind up in an emergency room. The cost of being treated that way is extremely high, and paid for by people who have insurance.

The United States doesn't generally let people die on the streets, but delivering health care to the poor and uninsured is far more expensive than for people who are insured. It's not necessarily an argument for a national insurance plan, just the result of a variety of choices the country has made over time that a lot of people end up getting very expensive health care that needn't be so expensive.

COVID-19 drew a line under the distinction. When the pandemic hit, hospitals saw more patients but were restricted from performing—demand also declined—elective procedures. Hospitals use high-dollar elective procedures to underwrite losses associated with their services to the uninsured and others who can't cover the costs of their treatments. When COVID-19 hit, the lack of elective procedures posed enormous challenges for hospitals. Many hospitals became financially distressed during the pandemic as their case loads shifted from revenue producers to emergency services. And while the new patient mix was similar to other countries, it took a bigger toll on U.S. hospitals and the U.S. economy than on other developed nations where hospitals are part of a national health program and reimbursed by the government for their costs. U.S. practitioners have jumped through those hoops for a long time, and been compensated for it, but COVID-19 magnified a weakness in the system.

Employer-Sponsored Health Care

After World War II, the U.S. tax code was changed to allow companies to deduct the cost of providing health care insurance for their employees. It quickly became an essential benefit for union shops, then generally across the board, employers buying into the scheme as an opportunity to split the cost of providing benefits with the federal government. Because employees were not able to deduct premiums they pay themselves, employer-provided coverage made economic sense for both sides. It was in some sense a quirky law—employers didn't get a tax deduction for providing home or auto insurance to their employees—and resulted in an odd break in the insurance markets. Many people get their health care coverage at work, but buy their own auto, home, and life insurance, even though everyone who drives is required to have auto insurance and anyone with a mortgage is required to have homeowners insurance.

Employer-provided insurance is working less well today because coverage is taking an increasingly large bite out of company profits. Companies are looking for ways out of those costs. But there's also the changing nature of work. Part-timers, freelancers, and contract employees don't have access to a company policy. Changes in how companies engage workers and changes in how people want to work are stressing a national system that relied heavily on employer-provided health care insurance.

From a global perspective, the U.S. system has put employers at a competitive disadvantage. Because all other developed nations offer government-provided health care as well as retirement and other social programs, foreign-based competitors operate free of some of those direct costs. The United States is also disadvantaged in terms of attracting foreign businesses. If you are an Italian firm thinking about establishing an offshore headquarters and deciding between Canada and the United States, you could be swayed by the fact that you won't have to pay for employee health care coverage in Canada like you would be expected to do in the United States. The U.S. firm does benefit by some tax differentials, but in Canada, the firm would avoid both the direct cost and the hassle of providing insurance through the firm.

The industry of medicine is changing dramatically in the United States to deal with the quirks of medical treatment financing. For one, large health care organizations that own hospitals are reallocating physician labor by employing doctors as "hospitalists," doctors who take over from the general practice physician once the patient enters the hospital. If you are a patient of a physician in one of the large health care systems, it is increasingly unlikely that you would see your primary care specialist once you enter the hospital. It's labor specialization and one way to add efficiencies—the pin factory come again.

Takeaways

- We enjoy improved health in part because we live healthier lifestyles. But life has also been lengthened considerably by improvements in medical technology and services.
- In evaluating health care spending, we need to distinguish between simple inflation in health services—simply paying more for the same thing—and an improvement in what we are buying that costs more.

- Sorting that out is compounded by the common practice of cost-shifting, whereby hospitals charge different clients different prices for the same treatment based on whether or not they have insurance, or if they do, what their insurance companies have negotiated with the hospital or other health care provider.
- If you are relatively well employed and well insured you enjoy some of best health care in the world and good outcomes. But for a large segment of the U.S. population that doesn't have high incomes and is not insured, outcomes are not good.
- Delivering health care to the poor and uninsured is far more expensive than to people who are insured.
- When COVID-19 hit, the lack of elective procedures posed enormous challenges for hospitals that became financially distressed as their case loads shifted from revenue producers to emergency services.
- Employer-provided insurance is working less well today because coverage is taking an increasingly large bite out of company profits.
- From a global perspective, the U.S. system of employer-sponsored health care coverage has put U.S. employers at a competitive disadvantage.

Equilibrium

Health care is a large and growing share of the economy. The U.S. population is aging, in part because health care technology has improved and lengthened lives. In turn, maintaining longer lives requires increasing health care expenditures. Health care provision is also politically contentious. In the United States, health care finance is usually a private sector matter until the individual reaches a certain age when the government then assumes most of the insurance burden through Medicare. While private insurance and the provision of health care has produced excellent results for people who can afford the insurance (often subsidized by employers, unlike most other types of insurance), covering the costs of the uninsured has been problematic.

It is also difficult to determine whether a change in the cost of a health care treatment is because it is a better treatment or due solely to health care price inflation. Health care spending has increased substantially, and outcomes are generally better. Distinguishing quality improvements from other price movements makes assessing health care costs difficult.

CHAPTER 23

First Fridays: Monthly Job Reports

Each month, typically the first Friday, the U.S. Bureau of Labor Statistics (BLS) releases its Employment Situation Report. More commonly known as the "monthly jobs report," the BLS release is probably the single most telling indicator on the state of the U.S. economy. It is our most meaningful economic diagnostic tool, fundamental to determining whether current expectations and economic forecasts are on track.

The monthly Employment Situation Report contains a great deal of data, but the two figures that command the most attention and move markets are the number of jobs added to the economy and the current top-line unemployment rate.

The "Noisy" Metric

The U.S. economy is characterized in one very important way by an enormous churn in the labor market. The net number of jobs created on a monthly basis is an important indicator of contemporaneous economic conditions. In terms of monthly data releases, it is hard to find one more important than the Employment Situation Report; it is the cornerstone of high frequency data regarding the economy, and the number of jobs created is central to that.

Still, new jobs numbers are "noisy." Any single month's numbers can be much ado about little—and the numbers get revised, although given the size of the labor market churn, revisions are comparatively small. Job creation numbers should be viewed through a longer lens (See Figure 23.1).

Prior to COVID-19 and the associated plummeting employment numbers, the U.S. economy had been adding on average a couple hundred thousand jobs monthly, growing a little faster than the labor market overall and pulling down the top-line unemployment rate. The disturbance in

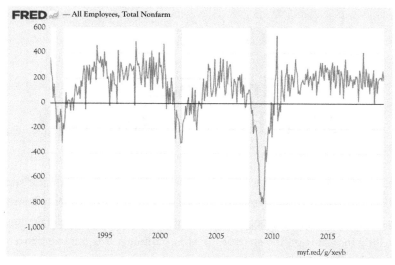

Figure 23.1 Number of U.S. jobs added or subtracted monthly for the 30 years ending December 2019

Source: U.S. Bureau of Labor Statistics

Release: Employment Situation

Units: Thousands of Persons, Seasonally Adjusted

Frequency: Monthly

All Employees: Total Nonfarm, commonly known as Total Nonfarm Payroll, is a measure of the number of U.S. workers in the economy excluding proprietors, private household employees, unpaid volunteers, farm employees, and the unincorporated self-employed. The measure accounts for approximately 80 percent of the workers who contribute to GDP. The chart shows the number of U.S. jobs added or subtracted every month for the 30 years ending December 2019

U.S. Bureau of Labor Statistics,

All Employees, Total Nonfarm [PAYEMS],

retrieved from FRED,

Federal Reserve Bank of St. Louis;

https://fred.stlouisfed.org/series/PAYEMS,

October 31, 2020.

the labor market from COVID-19 was unprecedented, unlike any other in our lifetime (See Figure 23.2). The shock in the early part of 2020 was so large that illustrating concepts with historical data is difficult when the COVID-19 time period is included.

The worst month in the Great Recession saw about 800,000 jobs disappear. In one month early in the recovery, the United States added about a half-million jobs, and thereafter bounced along adding jobs at that near-two hundred thousand average. As of the end of 2019, we were functionally at full employment, but still managing to hire at a good pace.

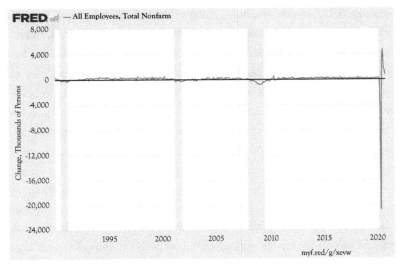

Figure 23.2 COVID-19 vs. the Great Recession

Figure 23.2 repeats Figure 23.1 with the addition of the months of 2020 through September. Everything illustrated by the first slide has turned into what is essentially a flat line close to zero. The Great Recession is one of the few places where the line deviates from zero, but it doesn't look all that awful—and it was the worst recession since the Great Depression. The job losses in April 2020 dwarf anything that had happened in the previous 30 years (and more), making even the years of the Great Recession look stable, though we know they weren't.

Source: U.S. Bureau of Labor Statistics

Release: Employment Situation

Units: Thousands of Persons, Seasonally Adjusted

Frequency: Monthly

U.S. Bureau of Labor Statistics,

All Employees, Total Nonfarm [PAYEMS],

retrieved from FRED,

Federal Reserve Bank of St. Louis;

https://fred.stlouisfed.org/series/PAYEMS,

October 31, 2020.

In fact, the labor market, while quite dramatic, is far from the only economic data series that was severely disrupted by COVID-19. It will complicate discussions regarding economic history for decades to come.

The "Tricky" Metric

Unemployment rates are key economic indicators, but using them can be tricky, mainly because there are more than the one most commonly reported rate. The BLS monthly reports include six different measures of unemployment, not so cleverly titled U1 through U6. The rate that gets the most attention is U3, the definition of which students of Economics 101 memorized as "the share of the labor force that has been looking for work recently but can't find it." To calculate U3, you divide the number of people who have actively sought work within the past four weeks but did not find it by the total number of people available to work (most of whom are going to be currently employed). At the outset of pandemic, early in 2020, that figure had worked its way down to 3.5 percent, essentially full employment as defined by economists. (A rule of thumb is that a rate of less than 5 percent signals a very healthy labor market, functionally at full employment.)

Those monthly figures, in particular the updated U3 unemployment rate, move the financial markets because they capture both labor demand and labor supply, the combination of which best illustrates activity in the economy. When businesses are aggressively hiring and the unemployment rate is low it's a sign the economy is doing well. At the same time, the labor supply reflects consumer preferences regarding jobs and income; the labor force will expand or contract based on consumers' current financial conditions and expectations of the future. At some point everything has to manifest itself in one of those two components; everything that happens in the economy touches the labor market and the unemployment rate measures both sides.

There will always be people looking for work because of a mismatch in the labor market that prevents everyone from having a job. They can be considered victims of frictional unemployment, where workers are in the wrong place or have the wrong skills, which is inevitable as jobs and the skills required to do them are constantly changing. So the U3 rate alone is insufficient as a true employment metric, even if it is the best measurement of the lot.

U6 is the broadest measure of labor under-utilization. Also released in the monthly Employment Situation Report, it includes an element of labor market dynamics that has become progressively more important in recent years. U6 counts everything that is in U3 headline rate plus two additional components: discouraged workers and people who are "part-time workers for economic reasons." If you are unemployed and get discouraged and stop looking for work for four weeks or longer but would take a job if one became available, you're not counted in U3 because you aren't actively engaged in a search for a job. Typically the number of discouraged workers varies with the business cycle. During a recession with high unemployment, we see more discouraged workers who assume, probably correctly, their job search efforts will go unrewarded.

A common complaint about the Employment Situation Report is that it doesn't capture a large segment of the labor market; it does, just not in the headline U3. Discouraged workers are captured in BLS surveys and included in U6. U6 is reported in the same monthly BLS press release; it's just not usually featured in media reporting.

The number of "part-time for economic reason" workers increased in the early part of the twenty-first century, soared during the Great Recession, and remained elevated, at least until the COVID-19 disruption (See Figure 23.3).

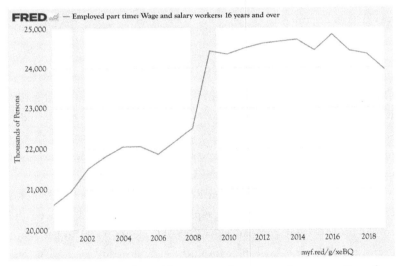

Figure 23.3 The number of "part-time for economic reasons" workers soared during the Great Recession and have remained high

Source: U.S. Bureau of Labor Statistics

Release: Weekly and Hourly Earnings from the Current Population Survey

Units: Thousands of Persons, Not Seasonally Adjusted *Frequency:* Quarterly

Wage and salary workers are workers who receive wages, salaries, commissions, tips, payment in kind, or piece rates. The group includes employees in both the private and public sectors but, for the purposes of the earnings series, it excludes all self-employed persons, both those with incorporated businesses and those with unincorporated businesses. For more information see https://bls.gov/cps/earnings.htmThe series comes from the 'Current Population Survey (Household Survey)'The source code is: LEU0264466800

U.S. Bureau of Labor Statistics,

Employed part time: Wage and salary workers: 16 years and over [LEU0264466800Q], retrieved from FRED,

Federal Reserve Bank of St. Louis;

https://fred.stlouisfed.org/series/LEU0264466800Q,

October 31, 2020.

The people who fill part-time jobs fall into two classes: those who prefer part-time work, known as "part-time for non-economic reasons," and those who would take full-time employment if they could get it, identified as "part-time for economic reasons." Gen Xers and millennials in particular are driving the noneconomic part-time segment of the labor force higher, but neither of the part-time worker groups is counted in U3. The "part-time for economic reasons" are included in U6 because they receive wages on a regular basis, even though they would like to be more actively engaged in the labor market. While they aren't technically unemployed, they are underutilized. People working "part-time for non-economic reasons" are considered content in their current state, and are not counted in U6 as underutilized.

A Widening Gap

Traditionally most unemployment rates move in the same direction. If you were reporting on unemployment, the U3 top-line rate would be sufficient. You didn't really need to look at the others because all their movements told essentially the same story. But the Great Recession blew up the relationship between U3 and U6.

In the latter part of post–Great Recession expansion, with U3 at historic lows, wages weren't growing rapidly, which we would expect at full employment because companies have to offer better wages to get people into the workforce. One explanation: the gap between U3 and U6. Neither discouraged workers nor part-time workers wanting full-time work demand higher wages to provide added labor. Discouraged workers want a job and part-time workers want more hours, and both are willing to hire on at prevailing wages. Wages started edging up toward the end of the post–Great Recession expansion as the gap between the two measures was starting to close. Then it blew up again with the arrival of COVID-19 (See Figure 23.4).

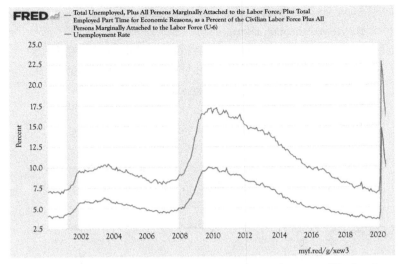

Figure 23.4 With the Great Recession, the gap between U6 (top) and U3 (bottom) unemployment rates widened, then narrowed, then widened again with the arrival of the COVID-19 pandemic.

Source: U.S. Bureau of Labor Statistics

Release: Employment Situation

Units: Percent, Seasonally Adjusted

Frequency: Monthly

The series comes from the 'Current Population Survey (Household Survey)'
The source code is: LNS13327709

U.S. Bureau of Labor Statistics,

Total Unemployed, Plus All Persons Marginally Attached to the Labor Force, Plus Total Employed Part Time for Economic Reasons, as a Percent of the Civilian Labor Force Plus All Persons Marginally Attached to the Labor Force (U-6) [U6RATE],

Retrieved from FRED,

Federal Reserve Bank of St. Louis;

https://fred.stlouisfed.org/series/U6RATE,

October 31, 2020.

Takeaways

- The Employment Situation Report, more commonly known as the "monthly jobs report," is the single most telling indicator on the state of the U.S. economy.
- The two report figures that command the most attention and move markets are the number of jobs added to the economy and the current top-line unemployment rate.

- New jobs numbers are "noisy." Job creation numbers should be viewed through a longer lens.
- U6 is a broader measure of labor under-utilization than U3. U6 counts everything that is in U3 plus two additional components: discouraged workers and "part-time for economic reasons" workers.
- Part-time for economic reasons workers widened the gap between U3 and U6 during the Great Recession.
- The gap was closing at the end of the post–Great Recession expansion but blew up again with the arrival of COVID-19.

Equilibrium

The monthly Employment Situation Report deserves, and gets, a great deal of attention because labor is central to virtually all economic activity. Changes in the number of people employed reflect changes in income that have implications for future spending and economic conditions. The monthly reports also reflect the condition of firms that will adjust employment to reflect current and near-term expected economic conditions. The unemployment rate moves as a function of both labor supply and labor demand, each of which individually reflects deeply fundamental conditions in the economy, and together contain an enormous amount of information that can be used to forecast the economic future.

CHAPTER 24

A Shrinking Workforce: Jobs and Work in the Twenty-First Century

In *The Rise and Fall of American Growth* (2016), Robert J. Gordon described a century of rapid economic growth fueled by technical innovations, one of the most important being the development of various forms of engines that created propulsion without the aid of moving water. That it was technically feasible to move goods off water, or to make goods without the power of moving water, had widespread implications for the U.S. labor market, including a decreased demand for human muscle. The new engines did work that previously required people and animals: tractors, and later trucks, replaced those original "teamsters," teams of draw horses and mules. The engines displaced droves of relatively unskilled workers. The engineers of the day skilled in water-based propulsion and mechanical systems remained employed, but the real action, and income, was reserved for engineers that could get engines not powered by water to work.

The same kind of shift is evident today in the move away from mechanical to electronic devices. We still need people who can build and fix machines, but the real action is in electronics that didn't exist twenty years ago. The divergence in skills as technology has evolved has mimicked that previous-era divergence in incomes when those with preindustrial labor skills didn't see their incomes grow while those who knew engines did. The gap in incomes grew wider following the Civil War through the Great Depression, nearly seventy years of stagnant wages for a large segment of the U.S. economy. All the real wage growth showed up in a relatively elite segment of the economy that could manage the new technologies. Just as is happening today.

Bye Bye Boomers

In fact, hourly wages for low-skilled U.S. workers had started to move higher right before the onslaught of the COVID-19 pandemic. Gains were in large part tied to a strong economy coupled with a shrinking workforce growth rate brought on by the retirement of the so-called baby

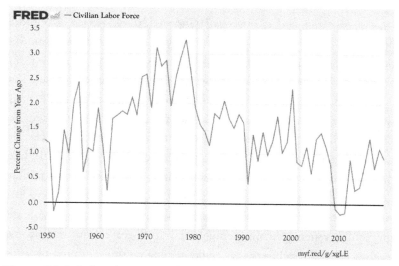

Figure 24.1 Labor-force growth peaked in the mid-1970s and has declined since.

Source: U.S. Bureau of Labor Statistics

Release: Employment Situation

Units: Thousands of Persons, Seasonally Adjusted

Frequency: Monthly

 Persons 16 years of age and older. The series comes from the 'Current Population Survey (Household Survey)'The source code is: LNS11000000

 U.S. Bureau of Labor Statistics,

 Civilian Labor Force Level [CLF16OV],

 Retrieved from FRED,

 Federal Reserve Bank of St. Louis;

 https://fred.stlouisfed.org/series/CLF16OV,

 October 31, 2020.

boom generation. The birthrate explosion in the decade following World War II produced a huge bulge in the workforce, but since the boomer birth years, generally considered 1946 to 1964, the U.S. labor force grew less rapidly (See Figure 24.1).

While the increasing rate of retirement of human capital is unique to the postwar period, other economies are experiencing the same shift. It is not yet history, not yet complete. We don't know how it will impact long-term economic growth. But we do know that we get growth in the economy by adding workers, and by making workers more productive through investments in physical capital, human capital, and new technology. A slower pace of labor-force growth is likely to slow economic growth as measured by GDP.

Further challenging the economy is that the boomers are as a group relatively skilled, having accumulated a lifetime of experience.

In addition to slowing real output growth, maintaining the income of retirees will present challenges as the ratio of retirees to workers rises. There is real concern about the ability of institutions, both government and private, to meet their obligations with respect to the increasing number of retirees who will need to retain their share of income through their increasingly longer lives. It is a problem that wouldn't have arisen had the labor force continued to grow at its previous pace. We're in a difficult position at the same time the nature of labor demand is changing, which is increasing the bifurcation in the labor force, hollowing out a middle class that includes middle managers who were paid well for what is now considered rather routine industrial-style work in favor of workers skilled in emerging technologies.

Despite technology's evident enhancement of productivity, the United States was functionally out of workers going into the 2020 recession. According to the Bureau of Labor Statistics, there were more active job openings than workers actively seeking jobs. The lack of workers was reflected in historically low unemployment rates. The only reasons for being unemployed were labor market frictions, that is, people with the wrong skills or in the wrong locations. The lack of needed skills was across the board, and the fact that the wages of low-wage workers were growing at a faster rate than wages on average was a clear indication that labor markets were tight all over.

The Immigration Wild Card

Immigration, both historically and today, is another labor force wild card. Despite the call for tired and huddled masses, the United States has gone through periods of being not so welcoming to immigrants, both to people who came unwillingly from Africa and Asia and willingly from European countries like Ireland and Italy. Our history is rife with issues of discriminatory practices and the related, ongoing social problems. Still, all those surges of immigrants added to our labor force and to the growth of the U.S. economy.

The in-migrations didn't always perfectly match the expanding needs of the labor market, but they did make up for labor shortages in an economy that was growing rapidly. Today we again see a real bifurcation in arriving immigrants, from the high-skilled, highly educated to the low-skilled, poorly educated. Given our shortage of natively produced workers, both are finding employment—in different areas, but employment nonetheless.

While how we deal with rationalizing immigration policy is a twenty-first century political hot potato, it is not an unusual challenge for the United States. We have struggled with immigration policy for a long time, even though in many cases, most cases, the economy needed the additional workers.

The prevailing question remains: Will the United States address the slowing growth of its labor force with immigration or accept slower long-term economic growth?

Takeaways

- We still need people who can build and fix machines, but the real employment action is in electronics that didn't exist twenty years ago.
- The gap in incomes, or income inequality, grew wider following the Civil War through the Great Depression, nearly seventy years of stagnant wages for a large segment of the U.S. economy for reasons similar to what we are experiencing today.

- Hourly wages for unskilled U.S. workers had started to move higher right before the onslaught of the COVID-19 pandemic. Gains were in large part tied to shrinking workforce growth brought on by the retirement of the baby boomers.
- Despite technology's evident enhancement of productivity, the United States was functionally out of workers going into the COVID-19 recession.
- We see a bifurcation in arriving immigrants, from high-skill, highly educated to low-skill, poorly educated people. Given our shortage of natively produced workers, both are finding employment.
- Will the United States address the slowing in growth of its labor force with immigration or accept slower long-term economic growth?

Equilibrium

The growth of the labor force is fundamental to overall economic growth, but how we manage it is frequently problematic. Slowing rates of labor-force growth suggest that the tight labor markets of the late 2010s will be a recurring issue causing problems for firms that need workers, as well as for a relatively increasing share of the population that is retired and dependent upon existing workers to maintain their standard of living. As well, the changing nature of the labor being demanded has led to some income distribution issues, a not-so-uncommon occurrence in U.S. history. Immigration can be and has been a significant source of additional workers for the United States, but immigration is a complicated political issue and a common issue of debate.

CHAPTER 25

Wages: Minimum and More

Ice cream cones and the economic theory on wages are a lot alike. The first ice cream cone you eat tastes great, the second, good but not as good as the first, and the third not as good as either of the first two—and you might be inclined to stop eating ice cream for a while.

At the root of economic thinking about wages is the theory of diminishing marginal returns: as a firm adds workers, each worker will add value to the output of the firm, but less value than the previous one. Returns in terms of output diminish with each additional worker. At the pin factory, two or three people making pins are more productive than one, but once you get to the fourth or fifth worker you get more pins but not as many per pinmaker as before. The theory implies that a firm will employ workers up to the point where the last worker added is contributing the same value to output as the wage that worker earns. In general workers should add more value to the output than they are being paid in wages, so firms are better off adding up to the point where the last one, the marginal one, brings in no profit, then stop hiring.

Of course not all labor is alike and not all jobs are alike. Still, the logic of the principle remains that faced with a particular wage rate, a firm will hire up to a point where more workers don't add profit.

To Minimum or Not to Minimum

Workers are supplying labor and will supply more if wages are higher, and firms want to employ more workers to get more output and profit. But firms are faced with diminishing marginal productivity. So it is at the intersection of supply and demand where the value of the marginal product equals the marginal willingness of workers to work at that rate.

That is the equilibrium wage rate that would naturally prevail in the labor market.

While that description of a competitive labor market is fairly clear, if labor is relatively abundant, the resulting wage rate may be quite low, low enough that there may be social pressure to impose a minimum wage. There should be a minimum wage, proponents insist, because there should be some minimum reward for work.

The argument *against* a minimum wage contends that if you impose a minimum wage above the wage that would naturally occur, employers won't be willing to hire as many workers. Businesses would need to cut back hiring to retreat back up the curve of diminishing value of marginal returns. The minimum wage, the argument goes, has produced an increase in the quantity of labor supplied and a decrease in quantity of labor demanded—and therefore, an increase in unemployment. In the simplest terms, by raising the price of an input you should expect a firm to use less of it, so raising the price of labor will result in less employment.

The argument *for* a minimum wage begs you to understand the reality that labor markets are more complicated than as defined by simple, generalized examples of behavior in competitive markets. Consider the situation where labor is not sensitive to wage rates. People who need money will take what they can get because they are not in position to influence their wage rate; employers have market power beyond that assumed by the simple competitive market model. Another way to look at it: Labor markets aren't necessarily like other commodity markets, and imperfection and distortions in the labor market can be quite large. Increasing the minimum wage might be appropriate in cases where there are market distortions—a large employer in a small town has undue market power and workers have very little market power—with results that would defy the simple competitive market theory.

The Effects of a Minimum Wage

The federal minimum wage hasn't changed since 2009, so adjusted for inflation, the real minimum wage has been falling gradually for more than a decade. In response, some states have imposed local minimum wages higher than the federal minimum. The variation in minimum wages is often a critical component in empirical studies of the effects of a minimum wage on the economy—and the results are mixed.

Much of the evidence turns out to be sensitive to the specifications of the test. In some cases, the evidence suggests an increase in the minimum wage will boost employment, get more people hired. It is not commonly the result of the studies, but sufficiently frequent that it deserves respect. The argument is that people working at minimum wages are "liquidity constrained"—that is, broke. They spend whatever they make. If there is a distortion in the labor market that would allow employers to pay higher wages but they don't, forcing a higher minimum wage means workers making more will spend more than before and the stimulus will lead to more employment. It is a controversial argument but there are studies to support it.

The most common result of studies, as reported in empirical literature, is that it's hard to make the call. Labor markets are complicated. In some of the states and cities, an increase in the minimum wage did not generate additional unemployment. But other issues complicate the story. For example, the movement toward locations with higher minimum wages in the 2010s occurred against a background of a very tight labor market. We could have expected wage increases anyway, as the functional market minimum wage was above the federal minimum due purely to tight market conditions. Where that is the case, the increase in the minimum wage won't lower employment, because the market is running ahead of the regulation.

Overwhelmingly, the empirical results with regard to a minimum wage are mixed. That by itself should be cautioning. It is surprising that empirical results aren't nearly as clear as theory. After all, the logic of an increased price leading to less demand for a particular product is sound. But both sides of the argument would agree that because the labor market is more complex than a simple test can capture, it's more important to understand what's happening beneath the surface. Tests of models can only determine so much, and given the complexity of the labor market it is relatively easy to find some fault in the design of a study producing results you don't like.

Impact of COVID-19

The 2020 pandemic put a new twist on the labor market, and consequently, wage data. The Bureau of Labor Statistics' monthly Employment Situation Report includes the number of hours worked and average wages of those workers. When the pandemic first struck the labor market, we saw an unprecedented number of layoffs, but also, and somewhat counterintuitively, a large increase in the prevailing hourly wage. Despite the layoffs, average hourly earnings increased because the layoffs were not uniformly distributed. They were concentrated in low-income jobs. Relatively high-skilled, high-wage people kept their jobs. So the mix of employment shifted the average wage upward substantially, not because anyone was getting paid more, but because those on the lower end of wage distribution lost their jobs.

Symmetrically, the pandemic will have a perverse effect on employment data for years. As the economy returns to normal, wage data will look depressed because of the composition of the returning labor force. The employment gains in the lower wage segment of the workforce will result in a reduced average wage.

Takeaways

- The theory of diminishing marginal returns as it applies to labor: as a firm adds workers, each worker will add value to the output of the firm, but less value than the previous one.
- The argument against a minimum wage contends that it produces an increase in the quantity of labor supplied and a decrease in the quantity of labor demanded, and subsequently, an increase in unemployment.
- The argument for a minimum wage begs you to understand the reality that labor markets are much more complicated than as they are defined by more simple and common examples of behavior in competitive markets.
- Both sides of the minimum wage argument agree that because the labor market is more complex than a simple test can capture, it's more important to understand what's happening beneath the surface.

Equilibrium

The labor market is central to the existence of any economy. A society needs to use its labor to make the products and services it wants. If we think of labor as comparable to any other input, then a minimum wage, which increases the price of labor, should decrease the amount of labor used. But minimum wage laws are often motivated by the notion that working in a society should be rewarded at least at some minimum level, and that the market for human time (labor) is fundamentally more complex than for other goods. The debate over minimum wages has many motivations, and the empirical literature faces a daunting task trying to model and test behaviors and conditions with precision in all the dimensions of the labor market.

CHAPTER 26

Measuring Prices: How Much Is a Dollar?

Measuring the labor market is tricky, but figuring out prices is downright befuddling. Of course, inflation is a core economic focus, but distinguishing between real and nominal movements in price makes calculating inflation something less than an exact science.

Even if inflation were at zero, prices would move relative to one another, that is, make real movements, like the price of peanut butter going up faster than bubble gum. Inflation is often thought of as a change in the value of money: the dollar is worth less today than it was last year or in 2010 or 1970, so both peanut butter and bubble gum would rise in price, regardless of their relative price movements. But prices change because supply and demand of one product compared to another change in real time, not only because of a change in the value of money. Technical innovation or constraints on supply may make some things popular and others obsolete. Real price movements occur continuously and need to be distinguished from price changes due purely to inflation—and that's where it gets complicated.

Cost of Living

Historically inflation has been thought of as reflecting changes in the cost of living. But your cost of living depends on what you buy. People differ in what they want or need to live. And their consumption bundles change over time. If all our consumption bundles were the same from one period to the next, inflation would be easy to determine: Compare the cost of spaghetti and iPhones and if the quantities are the same, look at the difference in what you paid this period versus last time.

In practice, however, your consumption bundle does change substantially over time, both because of your changing preferences and two critical considerations on the supply side: availability of more goods—there's something new to buy—and a shift to a lower-priced good or service of the same kind. The challenge then becomes comparing the goods or services in period one to period two. Has the cost of living changed if you paid less for something but it's not exactly the same good? You're paying less but getting less: a can of generically labeled green beans instead of name brand green beans.

Figuring inflation is even trickier when technical innovation comes into play. Consider automobiles. The Model T sold for five hundred dollars. You can still buy a car for five hundred dollars. It might be old and damaged, but it will go faster, drive farther, and otherwise outperform a Model T. We're paying a lot more on average for a car, but we are getting a lot more than before. How do you calculate inflation relative to automobiles when you have to take into consideration the advanced features in new cars? Similarly, we're paying a great deal more for health care but living longer, getting more for our money. Our consumption bundle has shifted, but adjusting inflation to consider quality innovations and technical advances is difficult; the advances can more than compensate for the change in nominal price.

Looking Back and Forward

If you are going to calculate inflation over the past fifty years, you have to consider the consumption bundles. If you start with what you bought in the 1970s and compare those prices to today's, today's are higher. A package of chicken that was two dollars is now ten dollars. The gas you paid three dollars a gallon for today was less than fifty cents a gallon in 1970. But if you start with today's bundle and look back, while the price of your chicken would have gone up, it would have cost tens of millions of dollars to have something that could do even some of what your two-hundred-dollar smartphone can do today, the computing power in even an early-generation smartphone being greater than the most sophisticated, multimillion dollar computer of the 1970s. In real terms, we have seen enormous *deflation* in what we are consuming; technology has dramatically reduced the costs for getting what we want.

Our consumption bundles change dramatically over a long period, which makes calculating real price movement difficult. The common proposition that what you bought for a dollar in 1970 would cost you six today is incorrect; price movement is ambiguous over time because we are switching our consumption toward things that are falling in price, like technology.

Chain Weighting and CPI Measures

Despite the ambiguity of measurement, inflation still happens. We usually measure inflation by putting together a consumption bundle at the beginning of a period and calculating the change in price to a next period, or looking back on a bundle we are consuming now. But as we have seen, this can be misleading, particularly if there is enough time between the comparison periods for the consumption bundle to change substantially. To address the ambiguity, economists now prefer a process called "chain weighting," which has become the default approach for calculating overall inflation in the GDP (the "GDP deflator").

The Bureau of Economic Analysis, an agency in the U.S. Department of Commerce that produces macroeconomic statistics, determines inflation by comparing prices for everything produced in one quarter to prices in the next quarter. Chain weighting, in effect, moves the base period forward with each new period. The change in the measured bundle won't be substantial overall, but using this inching along process provides a more realistic picture of inflation than talking about inflation in terms of 1970 or even 2010 dollars. Inflation is real, just difficult to calculate given the ongoing changes in products, services and bundles.

Since the concept of cost of living varies substantially with what you want to buy to conduct daily life, there are notable variations across different family situations in different locations. The Bureau of Labor Statistics addresses the variations by reporting on literally hundreds of different cost of living measures each month. Cost of living indices measure price movement for a consumption bundle for a litany of scenarios: an average family of four living in an urban area, an average family of three in an urban area, an average family of four in a rural area, a single head of household with three children, and all of these and more for each of seven BLS geographic areas, the four U.S. Census geographic areas, and all 50 states.

In addition to measuring prices of goods consumed, there are price indices for each of various stages along the production process: raw materials, intermediate goods, finished goods. If you're tracking costs of goods as they change, you can see what's pushing up or down prices at each step, such as a change in raw material prices showing up in materials, then intermediate goods, then in finished goods, then consumer goods. However, those producer price indices become less relevant as a predictor of overall inflation measurements as services claim a greater share of GDP, even if there are attempts at measuring service provider price inflation.

Retirement programs like Social Security and pension funds include cost of living adjustments, and many union contracts include provisions for cost of living wage adjustments. Most are tied to the Consumer Price Index (CPI). But the CPI does not necessarily capture the change in the cost of living for a particular household. In trying to compensate for changes in the cost of living, it will apply unevenly for, say, a retiree who owns their own home and is healthy versus a retiree who is renting and unhealthy. Both individuals will see their income adjusted by the same percentage, even though the change in their costs of living will be very different. Still, increases must be tied to some broad-based figure; there will continue to be winners and losers in cost of living adjustments.

Takeaways

- Distinguishing between real and nominal movements in price makes calculating inflation an inexact science.
- Real price movements occur continuously and need to be distinguished from price changes due purely to inflation.
- Historically, inflation has been thought of as changes in the cost of living. But your cost of living depends on what you buy.
- In real terms, we have seen enormous deflation in much of what we consume; technology has dramatically reduced the costs for getting what we want.
- Inflation is real, just difficult to calculate given the ongoing changes in products, services and bundles.

Equilibrium

Price level and inflation are central to thinking about the economy. But such simple concepts as inflation are very difficult to measure and can lead to very different assessments of changes in the value of the dollar over time. We need to be particularly careful when talking about long-term changes in prices, where the characteristics of the goods we consume may have changed dramatically.

CHAPTER 27

Productivity and Wages: What We Make for What We Earn

We get economic growth either by adding more workers to the labor force to make more goods and services or by making workers more productive. Both increase the size of the economic pie. When you add more workers, you have to divide the bigger pie by a bigger number of workers, but when everyone is more productive, everyone can, theoretically, get a bigger slice.

By extension, we talk about growing GDP as a means to improve our standard of living. But what matters in terms of a standard of living is not the size of GDP, but GDP per capita, which is a function of productivity. China's GDP is on pace to surpass that of the United States—in terms of purchasing power parity, China's economy is bigger already—but U.S. GDP per capita (about $65,000 in 2019) is much larger than China's (about $10,000 in 2019). In terms of its overall standard of living per person, China is still far behind the United States.

Productivity and the Standard of Living

The United States boasts one of the world's highest standards of living because of an incredible string of years of substantial productivity growth. In *The Rise and Fall of American Growth*, Robert J. Gordon pointed out that in the roughly hundred years from the 1870s to the 1970s, the United States was particularly good at applying new technologies, which allowed productivity to increase at a faster pace than most other economies.

The United States ended up with a high standard of living and a large economy. Gordon argued that a lot of the increase came from one-off advances in technology, like those land-based engines able to move manufacturing and other activities away from moving water. Consider communications. When telegraph wire was strung across the United States, the productivity gain over the Pony Express was of a much larger magnitude than the gain associated with the move from telegraph to video communications. Air travel had a huge impact on productivity when it was first invested in, but planes fly at about the same speed now as they did fifty years ago, even if the interiors are nicer and you can access the Internet from your seat. The biggest boost to productivity from the airline industry ended in the 1970s when they put jet engines on the planes. Since then productivity changes in air travel have been incremental.

It is productivity that allows for higher standards of living and wage gains over time. People benefit unequally from productivity gains, but without increased productivity there is nothing additional to distribute and no increase in the standard of living. As our nineteenth-century Italian economist Vilfredo Pareto would have put it, without productivity gains there is no way to make anyone better off without making someone else worse off.

Innovation and Investing

Productivity increases are driven by innovation and the United States has made huge investments in innovation. You could say we're all about technical innovation. (Gordon's argument that our big productivity gains are all behind us is controversial, if only because you never know what kind of technology will emerge next.) The United States is innovating and seeing productivity gains from its innovation, but it's hard to underplay the importance of the ongoing value of technological advancement and the investments that enable it.

Investing in new technology is a twofold initiative: in the research and development that will be the source of genuinely new innovation, then in implementing the new technology, making it work, and applying it broadly. Both efforts are expensive, which is why government gets involved in ways like grants, tax breaks, direct expenditures on national laboratories, and public–private programs like military labs and the National Aeronautics and Space Administration.

We've seen that emerging economies can grow rapidly by implementing old technologies that make them more productive because those technologies have established themselves as useful and are inexpensive to acquire and implement. Advanced industrial economies don't have that luxury. They have to invest in bringing new technologies to fruition. Part of the expense is in leading-edge technology that doesn't pay off. Like Sony's Betamax, which was superior technology to VHS, and even came to market earlier than VHS, but didn't catch on. Beta video technology looked like a winner and commanded a great deal of investment. That's part of the peril of investing in new technology but also part of the process of raising standards of living: the willingness to take risks.

Pin Factory Redux

Back at the pin factory you have been producing more pins by adding workers and will continue to add workers up to the point where the value produced by the marginal worker is just enough to cover their wages. But if a machine is invented that can automate part of the process and you implement that technology, the workers will be more productive on average than before. And if you add the machinery and your workers become more productive, you can pay them more both because the pin factory is more profitable and because the workers are more productive. Workers make investments too. They have to learn to use the new pin-making machine and are investing their human capital as they develop the skills and knowledge to make the new machine work.

As we've noted, human capital has become a bigger part of GDP in recent decades. As we shift to more of a services economy, more intellectual pursuits, physical capital investments have accompanied the investment in human capital. Authors need word processors to produce their intellectual property more expediently than when they used typewriters. While human capital grows its share of GDP, investment in physical capital is still required to make those services pay off.

Takeaways

- Investment in tangible and intangible capital is critical and will always be critical to advance the standard of living in an advanced economy.
- China's GDP will soon surpass U.S. GDP, but the U.S. GDP per capita is much larger. In terms of its overall standard of living per person, China is still far behind the United States.
- Productivity allows for higher standards of living and wage gains over time.
- Productivity increases are driven by innovation and the United States has made huge investments in innovation.
- While there is more emphasis on human capital in GDP, investment in physical capital is required to make those services pay off.

Equilibrium

In an earlier chapter, we discussed Keynes' notion that productivity gains would allow workers in advanced economies to enjoy a 15-hour work-week. That didn't happen. But the basis of that idea, that productivity enhancements would, over time, raise wages to the point where shorter hours would still support a good standard of living, may be true today. What we take to be a "good standard of living" seems to have kept pace with our productivity gains, even if the 40-hour week still remains the standard.

CHAPTER 28

Money Illusion: The Distinction Between Income and Buying Power

You're a U.S. citizen traveling abroad, in a spice market in Mumbai. Because you're not sure of the exchange rate, you don't have a good feel for whether what you're buying is expensive or cheap. How much *is* eight thousand rupees? You're trying to measure the cost in terms of dollars, but since the price is expressed in a currency you aren't familiar with, you can't immediately or easily make that judgment. What you are interested in is the real price of the product, but what you are told is the nominal price. The real price of the good is hidden behind the "veil of money" and seeing through that veil is not always easy.

The same can be true when the currency is familiar. Nominal prices change due to a host of reasons. If there is no inflation in the economy, the change in price of a good is a change in the good's real relative price. But if there is inflation, the prices of all goods are higher; the real price of the good you are considering could be unchanged.

Sorting out the meaning of changes in prices in an economy with an unstable price level can be tricky. Trying to determine when and how a real price has gone up or down, whether you're paying too much or getting a bargain in real terms, can be difficult even in your own currency.

Illusion and Inflation

The same applies to wages. Your paycheck is in nominal dollars. If you get a raise, how much of the increase in your nominal wages represents a real increase in your standard of living? If you're getting a 2 percent raise you might think you're 2 percent better off, but if inflation is 2 percent, you're real income is the same it was the previous year. You are a victim of "money illusion."

Even in an economy without a material inflation problem—the Fed has established 2 percent as an acceptable level of inflation—money illusion plays a big part in determining how you live where you live. In 1981, one of your authors, then living in New Orleans, received an offer to serve as editor of a magazine published in New York City. The nominal wage offered was substantially higher than what he was making in New Orleans, but when he traveled to New York to look for an apartment, he discovered his salary wouldn't even cover a one-room studio in Manhattan. The writer had to see through the money illusion to determine the real wage offer.

Money illusion is greater when inflation is substantial, but it still matters without inflation.

Employers and Money Illusion

People don't want to see their wages decline but sometimes it is appropriate, such as during an economic downturn where the circumstances are such that some level of employment can be maintained but only with workers taking a cut in compensation. Employers cut compensation in two ways. They can reduce your paycheck, which is tough to take—and tough to pull off as well, in particular when contracts and negotiations are involved. Another, and easier, way to reduce pay is to let inflation do it. If employees are being paid the same this year as the previous year, or even slightly more in nominal money but the increase doesn't compensate for overall inflation, they're getting a real wage cut. But it can be hard to see because of money illusion.

Sometimes money illusion can be useful. In the 1970s—years of double-digit inflation earned the period the moniker "the Great Inflation"—some employers were able to win real wage concessions by giving workers apparently nice nominal wage increases, but not enough to keep up with inflation. "A little inflation can grease the skids" was the oft-repeated expression, and money illusion the mechanism for employers to offer higher nominal wages and pay lower real wages. Money illusion was moving nominal prices on their products higher, but real prices were being cut, and employers needed accommodative wage concessions.

Of course people catch on when real income doesn't grow faster than inflation. That was story in the 1970s and 1980s, when cost of living increases in labor markets became standard. People saw through the money illusion created by the Great Inflation, that they didn't have as much buying power as before, and cost of living adjustments became a regular inclusion in compensation packages, including in pensions and Social Security.

The degree of difficulty measuring real versus nominal wages is similar to that of measuring prices. The real cost of living doesn't usually move significantly from year to year, although the nominal prices we pay may change notably, depending on inflation. Money illusion, while it is eventually transitory, is real and works to the benefit of some more than others.

Takeaways

- The nominal change in money prices might not fully reflect changes in real prices.
- Money illusion may be greater when inflation is substantial, but it still matters without inflation.
- Employers can cut compensation in two ways; reduce paychecks or let inflation do it.
- In the 1970s and 1980s, cost of living increases became a regular inclusion in compensation packages, as well as in pension funds and Social Security, as people generally saw through nominal price changes due solely to inflation.

Equilibrium

Economies express prices in their local currency. But what matters more is not the nominal price of the good, but its real price—that is, the price in terms of other goods or services that must be given up to make a particular purchase. If the real price of something changes, its nominal price will usually change. But if there is inflation, then sorting out the real price change from the nominal becomes difficult, particularly in the case of wages. We may jump at jobs that offer high nominal wages only to find out that in real terms that higher salary doesn't buy as much.

CHAPTER 29

Baumol Cost Disease: The Relationship Between Wages and Productivity

As we have seen, increases in productivity increase worker output, which in turn leads to potentially higher wages divided among more people and lower costs. It is how economies move forward. But there are some industries, in particular the live arts, where productivity gains aren't possible.

Consider a string quartet. Four people take the same amount of time to play a Bach fugue as when he wrote it in the early eighteenth century. You might be able to fit more people into a theater to hear it, but little else has changed. The pianist at Carnegie Hall playing a Beethoven piano concerto is no more productive than the pianist who played it when the Hall opened in the 1891. We have seen refinements in recording that have resulted in some productivity gains by distributing the music to large populations, but there have been no such gains for live performances— and not just music, but other performing arts, like dance and drama.

A Powerful Tool

In relative terms, the costs of live art are increasing because productivity everywhere else is driving prices down. The lively arts suffer the Baumol Cost Disease, named for William Baumol who developed the theory in the 1960s with William Bowen. Their concept is heralded as a powerful tool for understanding the modern economic world.

Baumol's intent was to better understand the economics of the arts, recognizing that symphony musicians weren't getting any more productive, but were making a lot more money than musicians playing the same pieces a hundred or so years earlier. Despite the lack of increased productivity, arts organizations had to raise wages to attract and retain the best musicians. If producers and facilities wanted quality performers, they had to offer wages that reflected the existing standard of living. And if increasing costs meant that live performances continued to grow relatively more expensive with no productivity enhancements, they had to charge more for tickets.

Continuing Rise in Prices

Baumol recognized that because you can't make the performing arts more productive, relative and real prices to attend performing arts events will continue to rise. In "real" terms, prices associated with live arts events have to grow faster than inflation.

The Baumol Cost Disease applies to other services, if idiosyncratically: some personal services, though typically one-offs, like haircuts and manicures, some forms of coaching, and other services that are essentially delivered one-on-one and cannot significantly benefit from automation. But we consider it particularly relevant to the performing arts because we think of the performing arts as a particularly vital part of our society. It is disturbing to see that live performances will continue to grow more expensive, if easy to understand why.

From musicians' perspective, the commitment and training associated with developing musical talent is much the same as it always has been as the real costs increase. Even if you're thinking casually about developing talent, costs are rising. Playing piano for the hell of it is getting more expensive as alternative uses of your time become more valuable.

Pandemic Acceleration

COVID-19 emphasized the significance of the theory and its implications. Broadway stages and Carnegie Hall are going to survive; they are as essential as arts venues can be considered. But most community arts companies rely on donors to support their activities. COVID-19 shut those activities down but it didn't completely eliminate the costs of maintaining those organizations. It was hard to convince fans to pay for music they weren't hearing or donors to contribute to organizations that weren't putting on performances. And when those community organizations and facilities reopened, they had to charge even higher ticket prices and face even greater challenges to recapturing their audiences.

Most important to understanding the Baumol Cost Disease is that there is nothing we can do about it. Some things are going to be increasingly expensive. We need the arts; they are fundamental to our existence. Arts organizations will have to beg for more and more money every year. Nonprofits in other fields that compete with the performing arts for funding may be able to achieve economies of scale and lower average costs, but Swan Lake will take the same number of dancers and rehearsals as when Tchaikovsky drew it up.

Takeaways

- For some industries, in particular the live arts, productivity gains aren't possible.
- Baumol Cost Disease: In relative terms, the costs of live art are increasing because productivity everywhere else is driving other prices down.
- In "real" terms, prices in these sectors have to grow faster than inflation. Because you can't make the performing arts more productive, relative and real prices to attend performing arts events will continue to rise.

Equilibrium

The Baumol Cost Disease is an example of the mechanics of equilibrium in the real world. The cost of attending live performances is going up in real terms, not because of some failure of the live performance industry, but because of productivity enhancements in essentially all other industries. Baumol's insight was that performing arts are stuck in terms of productivity, while almost everywhere else the output per worker has gone up. Increasing the standard of living for performers so they don't seek alternative occupations can't be the result of making the performers more productive, so it must come from higher real prices to attend their events.

CHAPTER 30

Exchange Rates and Purchasing Power

When traveling abroad, despite the challenge of translating an unfamiliar currency into a currency you know, you would think most real prices to be about the same once you apply the exchange rate. It might be twenty units of one currency for one of another, but in general, you expect purchasing power parity, that is, goods selling at the same real cost despite the currency.

In 1986, *The Economist* magazine created the Big Mac Index as a tool for examining purchasing power parity. For example, if a Big Mac costs $2.50 in the United States and the exchange rate of the dollar in British pounds is 1.25, you'd expect a Big Mac at the McDonald's on Old Kent Road in London to sell for two pounds. If the price of a Big Mac—the product was singled out due to its widespread availability and uniformity—is higher in one country than another after applying the exchange rate, the sandwich is relatively expensive, and that might be an indication that the exchange rate is likely to adjust to be more internationally consistent in terms of purchasing power parity. Of course, the implications of the Big Mac Index don't apply exclusively to hamburgers, but to a wide variety of common goods and services, such as labor costs and capital investment and rents associated with buildings.

The Big Mac Index is a representative measure and has worked somewhat well in determining what exchange rates should be. If a Big Mac is somehow mispriced in a local currency, the foreign exchange markets are likely to make a correction, even if in the short term it may be difficult to act on deviations from purchasing power parity, as, for example, there are considerable logistical challenges to moving goods from a low-price country to a high-price country. We don't expect the potential profits represented by a Big Mac in one country selling for more than in another to result in a large flow of Big Macs going from the low-price to the high-price country.

The engine that drives purchasing power parity is arbitrage—buying something in one currency where the price is low and selling it where it will command a higher price. The equilibrium effect on the global market is that arbitrage will drive the higher price down by making more of the good available in the high price market and the price in the lower price market will rise due to increasing demand. Eventually the two prices will have to be close enough together to make the buying in one country and selling in another unprofitable. The prices need not be exactly equal because costs like shipping are involved in the arbitrage. But theoretically, the two will more-or-less match.

Financial Markets and Arbitrage

Another, somewhat similar explanation for exchange rate movements is based on differences in returns on investments among different economies. One common way financiers use arbitrage is to buy and sell local currencies based on differences in local interest rates. If interest rates are high in a country, capital will flow there to get the higher return. If interest rates are low, capital will flow out. Where there is sufficient difference, the practice will drive exchange rates.

If a central bank or treasury wants to increase the value of its currency, it will push for higher interest rates domestically, which will increase foreign capital inflow and the demand for the domestic currency in foreign markets. For example, if rates in the United States are relatively high, we would expect the rest of the world to want to buy U.S. debt instruments. Since purchasing those instruments requires U.S. dollars, we would expect demand for the U.S. dollar to increase, pushing its relative value up against those currencies where domestic interest rates are lower. Unlike Big Macs, it is relatively easy to move money from one country to another. Equilibrium in exchange markets driven by financial markets should be a powerful determinant to exchange rate changes.

So now we have two fundamental ways of thinking about what determines a currency's exchange rate, financial market equilibrium and power purchasing parity equilibrium—and it isn't obvious why we would prefer one approach over another. Financial markets can move faster than goods markets, but goods markets represent the things we ultimately want to consume. And, as it turns out, neither is empirically particularly good for explaining exchange rate fluctuations.

Currency and Exchange Rates

A domestic policy maker wanting to increase the value of the country's currency can do so by raising domestic interest rates. But it's an imperfect method. International financial markets are noisy, even though money flows easily across borders, and are driven by many reasons, most of which do not involve arbitrages. Determining the reason behind exchange rate differentials is messy in practice.

The difficulties associated with exchange rate movements for international trade have often resulted in cross-economy pacts to fix exchange rates, eliminating the problem of possible changes in the value of a currency. We will look at the last grand experiment in globally fixed exchange rates in Chapter 34.

One approach to fixing exchange rates among countries that trade a great deal with each other is to move to a common currency, like the euro in the eurozone. Even though eurozone countries might enjoy some advantages sticking with their own currencies, those advantages are outweighed by the benefits, such as eliminating conversion costs across borders, of a common currency.

The arguments for free-floating exchange rates include allowing rates to change to better reflect the country's position against the rest of the world. If the country, for example, suffers some economic-related domestic disaster, changing the exchange rate would be easier than trying to change all the prices in the economy to adjust to the new internal normal. A fixed exchange rate could tie the hands of economic policy makers facing an economic challenge, one reason the world is largely operating under a free-market exchange rate mechanism.

As a very large economy with a common currency, the U.S. exchange rate is fixed domestically, even though states have very different economies. (The United States was often invoked in arguing in favor of a eurozone.) In the United States, the value of having a common currency far outweighs the disadvantages of not being able to adjust to some local financial disaster. Then look at Great Britain. Although it was a member of the European Union, it never did adopt the euro. In the end, that made Brexit a little easier to swallow. Having to reintroduce a domestic currency and reestablish the financial infrastructure necessary to deal with foreign exchange for routine transactions might have swung the decision the other way.

Takeaways

- A basic theme behind analysis of exchange rates is that in general real relative prices in different economies ought to be about the same, and the exchange rate between different currencies is what adjusts to make that happen.
- Purchasing Power Parity is expressed in terms of consumption of goods and services. *The Economist*'s Big Mac Index is an intuitive illustration of that concept in practice.
- Interest rate differentials can also drive exchange rate movements through capital flows. Capital will flow into a country with a higher rate of return, driving up the value of its currency.
- Exchange rate volatility is widespread, which makes it difficult to decide between fixed and free-floating rates as a preferred standard.

Equilibrium

We live in a world where countries using their own currencies want to trade with other countries using theirs. The rate at which one local currency is converted into the other is a central feature of international commerce. There are some very appealing explanations for why the relative values of currencies are what they are, and mostly they boil down to the idea that in real terms prices—and interest rates after taking into account risk and inflation—should be about the same. That can be hard to make happen in practice, particularly in the short run.

CHAPTER 31

The Fed's Job:
A Stable Economy

The primary directive and overall responsibility of most central banks is to maintain economic stability. It was instability that led to the Federal Reserve Act and the establishment of the U.S. Federal Reserve System in 1913. In response to bank runs and depositor panics, the Fed was created as a lender of last resort to banks when their mix of short-term liabilities and long-term assets had them temporarily illiquid.

Today's Fed has a dual mandate. It is charged by Congress with preserving price level stability but also maintaining maximum employment. The two goals often go hand-in-hand, although they can be in conflict, as was the case from the late 1960s through the early 1980s when both inflation and unemployment rose to and remained at uncomfortable levels. Confronted with such double trouble, the Fed had to choose: bring inflation down and risk a recession or stimulate the economy and allow inflation to rise. Under Paul Volcker, who became Fed Chairman in 1979, the Fed chose to tame inflation and take the recession. While the Fed took dramatic steps to provide liquidity and boost employment in both the 2008 and 2020 recessions, inflation was not an issue. The dual mandate has not presented much of a dilemma since the 1980 recession.

The Fed was challenged by the 2008 Great Recession, though not by banks. So-called nonbank banks, large financial institutions that were legally not banks but had balance sheets that looked like banks, found themselves in liquidity squeezes to the point the Fed had to step in to prevent widespread financial panic. While the liquidity provision was enormous, it was not accompanied by inflation. The United States was not alone in this situation. Many central banks provided extraordinary liquidity and worldwide inflation remained dormant.

A New Priority

Following the Great Recession, in the ensuing recovery and expansion, the economy was generally healthy. But not for everybody. While lower-income workers benefited by some wage gains, we also saw a notable increase in income maldistribution, much of it along racial lines.

Then came COVID-19. The pandemic was a natural disaster, not the result of an economic mistake. In the case of a natural disaster economic relief is often provided in the form of bridge loans to businesses that previous to the disaster were functioning well. Bridge loans are designed to keep businesses afloat until the economy gets back in shape. But early in the pandemic, no one knew how long the disaster would last; there was no way to know how to design bridge loan length.

Still, the federal government through the U.S. Treasury committed money in the form of loans over specified periods of time. Funds were also available in the form of COVID-specific grants, money that didn't need to be paid back. As well, the terms of the most widely used of the relief programs, the Paycheck Protection Program, allowed for loan "forgiveness" if the funds were used for payroll and other qualifying expenses like rent or mortgage payments, that is, to keep the business in business and the employees employed.

Meanwhile the Fed was in an odd position in terms of its mandate. The Fed only lends money; it has no power to distribute grants. Moreover, it doesn't loan money directly to businesses; it lends to financial institutions and supports financial markets. So to provide relief within its legal limitations, the Fed instituted the Main Street Lending Program, whereby it funded lenders to lend to businesses. The banks would lend and the Fed would assume the loans with guarantees from the Treasury. In essence, the Fed acted as a backstop for lenders, buying up loans they made to qualifying businesses.

Closing the Income Gap

While the Main Street initiative provided much needed funding to many small and mid-size businesses, the process of lending through financial intermediaries was faulted in that the money didn't reach many small businesses that didn't have established relationships with banks, especially small minority-owned businesses. The disproportionate distribution of the relatively low-cost loans served to call attention to racial inequalities in financial markets and the provision of financial services.

Recognizing the larger issues of income and wealth disparity and income inequality were related to the same fundamental causes that kept minority firms from participating on equal footing for disaster relief funds, the Fed changed its Longer-Run Goals and Monetary Policy Strategy. As noted by Fed Chair Jerome Powell in an August 27, 2020 press release, "Our revised statement reflects our appreciation for the benefits of a strong labor market, particularly for many in low- and moderate-income communities, and that a robust job market can be sustained without causing an unwelcome increase in inflation."

The release went on to address "significant changes":

- "On maximum employment, the FOMC emphasized that maximum employment is a broad-based and inclusive goal and reports that its policy decision will be informed by its 'assessments of the *shortfalls* of employment from its maximum level.' The original document referred to '*deviations* from its maximum level.'"
- "On price stability, the FOMC adjusted its strategy for achieving its longer-run inflation goal of 2 percent by noting that it 'seeks to achieve inflation that averages 2 percent over time.' To this end, the revised statement states that 'following periods when inflation has been running persistently below 2 percent, appropriate monetary policy will likely aim to achieve inflation moderately above 2 percent for some time.'"

The changes were subtle but meaningful. Inflation hadn't reached 2 percent since before the Great Recession and a tight labor market wasn't nudging inflation as might have been expected. Strong economic growth and low interest rates had benefited lower income workers to some degree following the Great Recession, and had served to make some progress against income inequality. So the Fed gave itself the option of keeping monetary policy eased until such time as inflation might become problematic.

The Fed, in essence, changed its policy to tolerating above-target inflation when there are some segments of the labor market showing appreciable stress. It would pay attention to slack in labor market segments in a way it hadn't before, explicitly looking at submarkets to address underperforming segments. The nuanced change made it more difficult for Fed watchers to predict the Fed's next moves, but also appeared an appropriate response to the realities of the post–Great Recession U.S. economy.

Takeaways

- The Fed has a dual mandate. It is charged by Congress with preserving price stability but also maintaining maximum employment.
- During the COVID-19 pandemic, the Fed was faced with legal constraints in its operations and instituted the Main Street Lending Program, whereby it funded lenders who would lend to businesses.
- The Fed's long-term response to the pandemic was to change its policy to tolerating low inflation when there are some segments of the labor market showing appreciable stress and looking at submarkets to address underperforming segments.

Equilibrium

Economic growth by itself is not acceptable in an economy where the results of that growth are disproportionately going to one segment of the society. There was an enormous influx of liquidity worldwide in response to a financial crisis in 2008, and it did not accelerate inflation. At the same time, tight labor markets were benefiting segments of the labor market that had not previously fully participated in the benefits of an expanding economy. The Fed's modified Longer-Term Goals allowing for more flexibility to continue favorable labor market conditions for underserved market segments, even if it means some compromise to inflation metrics, seems a reasonable response to the realities of the post–Great Recession U.S. economy.

CHAPTER 32

What the Financial Markets Reveal

Show me the charts and I'll tell you the news.
—Bernard Baruch, financier and economic advisor to
Woodrow Wilson and Franklin D. Roosevelt

Whenever we buy anything, two things happen: A good or service is flowing in one direction; financial assets are flowing in the other. The assets are typically money, but they could also be debt, such as the instant debt instrument you create when you use a credit card. That new debt instrument is a very small part of the larger set of financial markets, but it is nonetheless critical for the way transactions are conducted around the world, and collectively, consumer debt in its many forms constitutes a notable share of the credit market. Paying attention to what's happening in financial markets, not just stocks and bonds but any marketplace where securities are traded, will tell you what's happening in the real economy.

It's relatively difficult to monitor the flow of goods and services in real time. The global marketplace is so large and diffused that it's hard to keep track of all the carrots being bought in all the stores in all the world. But that's not the case with financial transactions. When you use a credit card to buy something, it is recorded in real time. In principle, this ability to see transactions in real time extends to the larger financial markets. When you used that credit card, someone, usually the credit card company, bought the debt you created. Those credit card companies need financing too. The financial markets facilitate those movements, allowing buyers and sellers to trade financial assets, providing returns for those with funds to loan to those who need the money. The example of consumer expenditures is a relatively minor part of the larger flow of financial assets, but an equivalent flow is true for all transactions, and everything that gets transacted at some point moves a needle in a financial market.

While equities markets can appear volatile, the broader, all-inclusive financial market, particularly the debt market, is fairly stable in the sense that the people participating actively in each market work to forecast inflows and manage outflows. Despite their enormous size and massive daily money churn, financial markets as a group usually are not characterized by extreme volatility. Financial markets are all about allocating resources and liquidity over time, and there is something to be gained by looking at what's going on in the financial markets because everything happening in real terms in the economy is having an equivalent transaction on the financial side of the economy. Hence, "Show me the charts and I'll tell you the news."

Information and Probability

When we think of financial markets, we think equities, the stock market, the Dow Jones or S&P 500, which reflect the ownership values of publicly traded companies. But the debt market is much larger, encompassing corporate debt and government debt as well as the various forms of consumer debt. It involves a great deal of trading, just like equity markets but on a larger scale and not through well-known platforms like the New York Stock Exchange.

Both the debt and equity markets are concerned about information that changes the outlook for the future of the companies, governments, even individuals issuing the securities. If the economy looks like it's getting better or worse, that will be reflected in equity prices and interest rates. An enormous amount of energy is dedicated by financial market participants to understand what the current flow of information means to the future course of the global economy. Because global markets are substantially entwined, changes in financial market prices reflect something like a global consensus on the meaning of the news.

The financial markets process a great deal of information continuously, which results in changes in stock and bond prices. That makes those markets volatile. The information is often ambiguous or uncertain. But while new information might not say something definitive about the future state of the world, it can at least change the probability of something happening—for example, when Pfizer announced in late 2020 that it appeared its COVID-19 vaccine would be effective. Very few things are certain, but financial markets respond to how probabilities have shifted based on new information—and Pfizer's information was very positive news because it suggested a higher probability of the pandemic ending sooner than we thought it would before the announcement.

Derivatives: New Instruments, Exceptions to the Norm

In late 2007, one financial market, the subprime mortgage market, seemed to be underperforming in terms of how the various financial models had expected it to behave. The subprime market was not a large percentage of the overall financial market for mortgages, but a number of "derivative" securities had been developed to finance those mortgages. A derivative security is a security that "derives" its value from another security rather than some fundamental underlying activity. Subprime mortgages were bundled together, and those bundles were then sliced up in a variety of ways, and the slices of those bundles were securities that derived their value from the performance of the bundle. Pricing these derivative securities required knowing something about how the underlying bundle of mortgages was going to perform, and various models were produced to project various aspects of the bundle's cash flow, which, in turn, was used as the basis for the price of the derivative securities.

But the subprime market didn't behave as the models had expected. The derivative securities constructed to synthesize the safe and stable debt instrument constructed out of some less-than-prime mortgages suddenly turned out to be not so safe and stable. Unexpected losses were being realized, and who was going to bear what share of those losses became a pressing concern. As a consequence, the prices related to the financial instruments associated with subprime real estate declined as doubts increased about models behind the derivatives.

Because many derivatives in other debt markets were structured in similar ways—think subprime auto loans or many forms of consumer loans—the essential mechanisms of many derivatives were called into question, and many who took for granted that flows would work the way they had predicted lost confidence in the models used to price the derivatives. Owners of other derivative securities worried about how vulnerable their markets were to the same kind of problems, even though the markets were different. (The subprime auto loan market behaved, if anything, better than expected during the 2008 recession; people needed their cars to get to work.) Again, it was an issue of probabilities, and uncertainty, by investors who had assumed the predicted prices were correct. What followed was a lot less certainty very quickly and substantial volatility in the financial markets.

Interest Rates and Expectations

Financial markets, because they reflect the collective judgment of everyone on the planet, contain an enormous amount of information, more than any one person could process, but collectively informing and reflecting the expectations of future income and consumption. People in emerging economies are saving based on economic conditions they are experiencing, but also on what they expect in the future, which is not limited to their economy but part of a larger view of what's going on around the world. Because capital can move across borders quickly, minor changes in the behavior of markets in one sector of the world can quickly propagate in others.

Global interest rates were low throughout the late 2010s and into the 2020s. Interest rates around the world were low, not based on the policies of industrialized countries' central banks, but as former Fed Chair Ben Bernanke observed, because of a glut of savings in the world. That glut reflects rising global income along with concerns and considerations about income flows, consumption and capital needs and expectations over time.

Consequently, we better pay attention to the financial markets, as in, "Show me the charts and I'll tell you the news."

Takeaways

- If you pay attention to what's happening in financial markets, you will get a consensus view of what's happening in the real economy.

- While equities markets can be volatile, the broader, all-inclusive financial market is stable, moving capital around to meet the current and future needs of the global economy.
- Very few things are certain, so what financial markets are responding to is how probabilities have shifted based on new information.
- Financial markets, because they reflect the collective judgment of everyone on the planet, contain an enormous amount of information, collectively informing and reflecting the expectations of future income and consumption.
- Interest rates around the world are low because there is a glut of savings in the world that reflects global concerns about income flows, consumption needs and expectations over time.

Equilibrium

Changes in financial markets reflect the collective judgment of an enormous amount of people. There is a duality between activity in the real economy and financial markets. Transactions are typically paid for with a financial instrument and, consequently, each transaction has some marginal impact on those markets. Moreover, longer-term decisions about savings and the allocation of those savings to various capital projects also weigh heavily on financial market conditions. And since capital can usually flow rather easily across economic and political boarders, players in these markets span the globe. Consequently, it's important to pay attention to what financial markets are trying to tell us.

CHAPTER 33

The Yield Curve: What Is It Saying?

The yield curve is one of the most telling and referenced of all economic indicators. It is important because it represents the collective judgment of all participants, investors, and borrowers in financial markets everywhere.

At the turn of the twentieth century, American economist Irving Fisher published an "equation" that is still used to understand nominal and real interest rate behavior. He proposed that nominal interest rates can be decomposed into two factors: one is a real return on investment and the other, expected inflation. The Fisher equation declares that the real rate of return on a loan should be the nominal interest rate plus expected inflation. The lender requires some real return for parting with their wealth for a period of time, and since the interest rate is in nominal terms, that nominal rate must reflect expected inflation in order to preserve the underlying real rate of return.

Risk, Inflation, and Real Return

Risk, inflation, and real return are the three major elements in determining the nominal interest of any given security or debt contract. The longer time frame you commit to in lending or investing your money, the more all those factors come into play. If you're lending overnight you're not concerned about inflation and probably not risk, only rate of return. But if you are committing to ten years, you want to be compensated accordingly, that is, at a rate of return greater than you would get tying up your money for one year and repeating the process over and over nine more times. Your ten-year commitment is not identical to ten one-year commitments because the lending terms can change in ways not possible in a ten-year commitment. Investment projects are fraught with risk, and there is a chance that whatever you are investing in will fail; the higher the risk of failure associated with the particular security the higher return you want.

Particularly in the private sector, risk increases over time. No firms currently in the Dow Jones listing were listed when it debuted in 1896. Even the greatest companies encounter problems over time, so the longer the investment period, the greater the risk and the higher the loan interest rate. Generally we want real rates of return to increase the longer the life of the bond, debt security, or whatever. Inflation could go up, down or stay the same over that period, which would move the nominal rate accordingly. Consider also that expectations about the underlying economy are not constant. If the economy is expected to strengthen in the future, then the demand for loans should increase as well and real returns will be higher when the economy does strengthen. But if the economy is expected to slow, loan demand, returns on investment, and inflation would all be expected to decline.

We typically look at U.S. Treasury securities when we talk about the yield curve. The Treasury yield curve is informative because it involves real returns and expected inflation and is not complicated by risk of default. We assume the United States will be around 30 years from now and paying off its 30-year bonds as they mature.

A Shape-Shifting Curve

The yield curve should slope upward. The further out in years you consider, the higher the interest rate and therefore the higher point on the curve. But there is a challenge in assessing what the yield curve suggests: figuring out the change in nominal rates decomposed into real return over time and/or inflation. It is a confounding complication—not so much the curve itself, but the changes in the curve that come about with new information. If employment numbers are good in a particular month the curve will steepen, given that it means the financial markets think the economy is getting better. When the news is not good, it will flatten. Inflation news can also change the slope of the yield curve, adding a degree of difficulty to determining whether it's more or less inflation or a real change in economic activity that we should expect in the future.

But we think of inflation and real activity as at least somewhat correlated: When the economy is humming you look for inflation.

Inverted Yield Curves and Distortions

If the financial markets expect a recession, projected interest rates will be lower and exhibited as a downward slope, the so-called inverted yield curve. If today yields are higher than in the future, that must mean that projected real returns and/or inflation will be lower. As such the slope of the yield curve is often used in economic forecasting. When it's steep, financial markets suggest the outlook is good; when it flattens, financial markets expect a recession. Empirically, the slope of the yield curve is a comparatively useful, if sometimes imperfect, forecasting tool for economic activity.

Yield curves can be distorted, in particular when interest rates get near zero, which will deliver negative real (after inflation) returns. Moreover, the "zero lower bound" on nominal interest rates has been broken. Financial market conditions during and after the 2008 financial crisis and during the COVID-19-induced recession pushed nominal interest rates below zero in several European countries. That you would have to pay someone to hold onto your money for ten years doesn't appear logical, as in, "I lend you money and at the end of the loan you pay me back less than I loaned you." This odd condition of negative nominal interest rates wasn't previously even a consideration, but it happened in Germany, noteworthy because it is a major industrial economy, and elsewhere in Europe.

And it complicated our interpretation of the U.S. yield curve. The United States is not likely to default on its debt. Nor is Germany, but if you put your savings in German government bonds you'll get back less money than you put in. Because global investors reasonably want to avoid a negative return, they will divert their capital flow into economies with at least non-negative nominal rates. Investors seeking holdings in the United States where they could get positive if tiny returns reduced interest rates further, creating a distortion in the U.S. yield curve. It also served as a warning to be cautious about interpreting the yield curve in historic context as we had never experienced negative interest rates.

Like other economic measurements, the yield curve is imprecise and far from perfect. But it is a powerful tool and generally has been a good predictor. As cautionary curve aficionados enjoy noting, an inverted yield curve has predicted nine of the last six recessions.

Takeaways

- The Fisher equation asserts that the nominal rate of return on a loan should be the real interest rate plus expected inflation.
- Risk, inflation, and real return are the three major elements in determining nominal interest for any debt security or contract.
- The curve itself is not usually an issue; it's the meaning behind changes in the curve.
- The slope of the yield curve is often used in economic forecasting. It is usually upward sloping and when it's steep, financial markets suggest the outlook is good; when it flattens or inverts, financial markets expect a recession.
- Yield curves can be distorted, in particular when interest rates get near zero, which will deliver a negative real return. Negative nominal rates further complicate interpretation of the curve.

Equilibrium

Investors and borrowers around the world form expectations about the economic future and commit their real money based on what they think outcomes will be. Their actions shape the yield curve. It is a simultaneous system of actions and expectations from a very large set of economic agents borrowing and lending, saving and investing, and collectively making judgments and acting in ways that are reflected in the yield curve.

CHAPTER 34

The Dollar Versus Everything Else

In July 1944, as World War II raged on, 730 delegates representing all 44 Allied nations gathered at the Mount Washington Hotel in Bretton Woods, New Hampshire. Following 22 days of deliberation, they agreed to a system of rules that would govern their currency exchange rates. The Bretton Woods Agreement essentially fixed the exchange rate for each of the 44 countries, limiting deviations to 1 percent and tying those exchange rates to the U.S. dollar in recognition of the United States as the world's leading economic power. As the "reserve currency," the dollar would be fixed to gold. The United States would be on the gold standard; all other Allied nations, on a dollar standard.

The Allies next set up the International Monetary Fund (IMF) to oversee the agreement. The IMF was not a central bank, though it could be a lender of last resort to a country experiencing transitory problems maintaining its exchange rates. But only on the condition that the borrower fix its imbalance. Because international trade imbalances are often caused by domestic trade imbalances, the IMF mandate included—it still includes—usually demanding austerity measures by governments taking its loans. Some of those borrowers have grumbled over imposed austerity, but not excessively as austerity has worked to cure imbalances.

Also emerging from the Bretton Woods negotiations, the Bank for International Settlements (BIS) was assigned the task of providing the accounting mechanisms that would allow the IMF participants to settle up with one another. Payments needed to more-or-less balance in a fixed exchange rate regime, and somebody had to do the accounting and the settlement of the international accounts. John Maynard Keynes, who headed up the British delegation at Bretton Woods, arranged first to save the BIS, established in 1930, from dissolution, then to take on its new assignment.

From Fixed to Free Market

Keynes championed the idea of fixed exchange rates, arguing that they provide businesses greater certainty in international transactions. If contracts were set under a specified rate, then the rate was later changed, it would devalue the proceeds from the contract for one party and increase the value for the other party.

But despite the stability mechanisms, periodic currency devaluations did occur in countries with varying degrees of economic trauma. In the 1960s, as Europe and Japan became more competitive with the United States in terms of output, a deteriorating U.S. balance of payments threatened an international run on U.S. gold, and in 1971, President Richard Nixon took the dollar off the gold standard, effectively replacing the Bretton Woods system with floating exchange rates determined by the free market.

Many smaller countries retain fixed exchange rates with their primary trading partners—if most of your trading is with one partner, a fixed rate makes sense—but by and large, major currencies are actively traded in global markets.

The dollar is still the default reserve currency, the dominant currency for international trade, though it's position has been challenged from time to time. When the euro was introduced at the turn of the century, it was projected to become at least an alternative reserve currency, which it has to some extent. Eurozone countries that trade most within the euro area have used the euro as a reserve currency along with the dollar. But a common currency requires the involved countries to coordinate fiscal policies, and that hasn't happened as euro advocates thought it would. Much like U.S. states, eurozone countries can't issue debt to finance operating deficits, and some have struggled to reduce deficits as required to get the euro to work as a default currency. Large economies like Greece and Italy might have addressed their imbalances by devaluing their currencies, but they couldn't do that with the euro. On the other hand, Great Britain's decision to hold on to its own currency and not adopt the euro made

Brexit, its withdrawal from the European Union, less cumbersome. The euro will continue as a dominant world currency, but for most central banks and treasuries the dollar remains the reserve currency.

The Chinese yuan poses some threat to dollar dominance. It has become the reserve currency throughout Asia as China's economy dominates that region of the world. But while it is seeing increased global use, it is still far from achieving status as a dominant global currency.

Cryptocurrencies

Cryptocurrencies' uniqueness is in their lack of association with any sovereign government. They depend on the confidence in their technical underpinnings. Their advantage is in how easily and quickly they can be used to move wealth anywhere globally. But they are not always welcomed by sovereign governments. Most governments want to be able to track transactions as they can usually do with transactions conducted in their own currencies. Because cryptocurrencies facilitate transactions outside the regulatory purview of sovereign states, they face regulatory restrictions in many countries where their ease of transaction is cause for suspicion.

Cryptocurrencies have yet to gain traction in large international business deals. Because they have no affiliation with any sovereign currency, they have no standing in any sovereign court and are treated as foreign currencies or commodities. The world's courts and arbitration systems are set up to resolve disputes in domestic currencies, not in cryptocurrencies. Given the global legal environment, cryptocurrencies are not likely to improve their share of use in large international transactions any time soon.

Takeaways

- The Bretton Woods Agreement essentially fixed the exchange rate for the 44 Allied nations, limiting deviations to 1 percent, and tied international exchange rates to the U.S. dollar.
- The International Monetary Fund often demands austerity measures by governments taking its loans.

- In 1971 President Richard Nixon took the dollar off the gold standard, effectively replacing the Bretton Woods system with floating exchange rates determined by the free market.
- The euro is a dominant world currency, but for most central banks and treasuries the dollar remains the reserve currency.
- Given the global legal environment, cryptocurrencies are not likely to gain traction in large international transactions any time soon.

Equilibrium

After World War II an international currency system that fixed exchange rates to the U.S. dollar made sense, especially if the dollar were then tied to gold. Providing some stability in exchange rates would promote international business and hence increase prosperity. But a few decades later, persistent imbalances led to the adoption of market-determined exchange rates as a way to maintain equilibrium in global markets. The dollar has remained the default global reserve currency even as contenders have begun to emerge regionally.

CHAPTER 35

Buy Low, Sell High:
Efficient Markets

It happens more often than not. The first question from the audience attending a talk on economics is, "What's the market going to do?" And invariably, the presenter is ready with the quip: "If I knew what the market was going to do tomorrow I wouldn't be here today." We might have longer-term views about asset prices but no one can predict how the market will move from one day to the next. The reason: Markets are "efficient."

In his 1973 book, *A Random Walk Down Wall Street*, Burton Malkiel explained how the efficient market hypothesis applied to investing, that security prices reflect the collective judgment of the full complement of investors in global financial markets, which includes everyone from highly paid specialists with extensive resources to unsophisticated investors buying and selling based on what they think they see. Malkiel contended that the current market price of a security is the appropriate price given all available information. The only thing that can cause a price to move, he offered, is news, and news by its very nature is unpredictable (if it was predictable we'd already know it and it wouldn't be news).

As a result, short-term movements in securities prices are functionally impossible to predict in a systematic way. They will behave in a manner identified by statisticians as "a random walk": If you take a random walk, you don't know which way you're going next. The best estimate of where you'll be is where you are now. You don't think you'll be where you are now, but there is no better estimate of where you'll be.

With a fourteenth edition released in 2019, Malkiel's book and its premise remain a foundation for modern investment advice, that you can't beat the market at any point in time because it moves only on news that is otherwise unpredictable. Some investment advisors might have a string of good decisions, even years of being on the right side of the market, but you wouldn't expect that statistically, and a string doesn't guarantee a prediction of a next outcome.

A Fool's Errand

Malkiel observed that over time the market offers positive returns on average. He suggested that trying to time the market is a fool's errand; it might work for a short period of time, but accidentally not systematically. If you have some particular piece of trading information on some security, someone else has already heard it. And you won't make better investment decisions than all those sophisticated and unsophisticated systems that combine to drive the financial market. As opposed to picking stocks, Malkiel advocated buying broad portfolio mutual funds with low management fees as a better investment strategy over the long run. Buy the market and hold it.

Wall Street wasn't operating like that when Malkiel's book debuted. There was a kind of prestige associated with putting your money in the hands of a pricey investment advisor. And certainly there were some advisors who did better than the market, but usually not for long. Successful managers' success worked against them. They attracted more and more money, and as they brought in more investment capital they became a bigger player in the market and an influence on the market itself as others adopted their strategies. They could no longer exploit inefficiencies in the market when they had become the market.

If there is a way to make above average profits for a while, it is self-destructive over time. The market will step in, see the unusually large rates of return and by adopting those processes remove their advantage by arbitraging them down to normal returns or bolstering the returns of the whole market. Unusual success attracts competition, which makes that success not so unusual. Either way the market will move back to where the price of a security reflects the collective judgment of the financial markets—and securities return to their random walk.

The efficient market hypothesis, and not insignificantly Malkiel's powerful text promoting it, spurred a number of financial innovations, in particular index funds, each of which is comprised of an "entire" market—the Dow Jones, the S&P 500, specific industry indices like energy or health care sector funds. They all reflect the recognition that buying and holding the market while paying the lowest possible fees produces a very good outcome over time, and that trying to beat the market by picking individual winners and losers is not going to be successful in the long run—maybe not even the short run.

Of course, there are challenges to the efficient markets hypothesis. But they exploit irregularities that come from maldistribution of information and regulatory obstacles and frictions.

We know that there are insiders who have access to information before others, and we've made insider trading illegal. Consider how various pharmaceutical firms announced their COVID-19 vaccines. They were careful with their press releases to share their results in a very public way to ensure the information was fairly distributed.

The efficient markets idea transformed the way we think about securities investing and the investment products offered by Wall Street. In the 1960s and 1970s, technical analysts would look at a pattern of a security's price over time and find patterns repeated. They plotted prices—it was largely before the wide availability of computers—and the emerging figures led them to determine how securities would perform. But Malkiel taught us that you can get the same patterns by flipping coins, that patterns emerge after the fact and don't provide reliable information about the future.

Joining the market with low-cost mutual funds has proven over time to be a successful investment strategy. It has also changed the financial advisory business. The current breed of advisors tend to be fiduciaries who seek to help their clients structure portfolios that accommodate their risk levels and understand their investment goals.

Takeaways

- The efficient market hypothesis tells us that the current price of a security is what it should be given all available information.
- Unless you can read the future you can't systematically beat the market.

- Joining the market with low-cost mutual funds has proven over time to be a successful investment strategy.
- The current breed of financial advisors are fiduciaries who seek to help their clients structure portfolios that accommodate their risk levels and understand their investment goals.

Equilibrium

The efficient markets hypothesis is a powerful example of equilibrium in action. Information is everywhere, and known by some. The collective actions of these information holders results in the collective judgment of the market regarding prices. As a result, it is very hard to do better than the overall market over time. To be sure, there can be errors, misleading or false information or individuals that have more information than others, but those defects and benefits don't endure. The market learns and adjusts. You can't beat the market over time; it's better to join it.

CHAPTER 36

An Expert Wife's Advice

"If you work half your life, save half of what you make." The formula for a comfortable retirement is the premise of a lecture on personal finance by Rosemary Cunningham, Ph.D., economist and professor at Agnes Scott College in Georgia. Her precept is: If you start earning in your mid-twenties, retire in your mid-sixties and live the average lifespan of a U.S. citizen, near 80, you will work half your life, so you will need to save half your earnings to maintain your standard of living in the other half.

There are nuances to the formula, including complications with contributions to and from parents and children, and influences like compound interest and rates of return on investments. Still, as a society, we don't come close to saving enough of our income during our working years.

Few of us would be willing or able to put aside 50 percent of our paycheck. But formula aside, we have fallen short on savings to the point we face a national dilemma, a dilemma that has emerged through a simultaneous change in both our work life and lifespan: equilibrium at play on a grand scale.

Life After Work

Social Security was instituted in 1937 as a backstop for people living unusually long lives. The retirement age, when you started receiving Social Security, was 65, but average life expectancy was less. You weren't expected to retire from gainful employment. You worked until you died, as had been the general rule through history. Saving for retirement then, in an intergenerational sense, is a relatively new phenomenon, something we've had to consider for less than a hundred years. A radical change of behavior over a couple of generations is possible, but it requires social-ization, and retirement was not a familiar concept that could be passed along with any degree of understanding based on experience until very recently.

Once life after work became the norm, many of us didn't worry about income in retirement. Just as we started getting our health care insurance from our employers after World War II, we had employer-provided pen-sions, defined benefit plans that delivered pre-established monthly pay-ments starting at retirement age and continuing to death. Between our pension and Social Security, and Medicare as of 1966, we would be taken care of in our golden years.

But our longer lives rendered defined benefit pension plans unafford-able for many employers. Funding for defined benefits proved inadequate to cover the burdens of an aging retired workforce that was living longer than the actuaries who set up the plans had envisioned. Pension obliga-tions bankrupted some firms. Some of the nation's largest firms had to reorganize not so much because their operations weren't profitable but because their pension obligations were so large they were no longer finan-cially viable under those arrangements. Prior to General Motors' bank-ruptcy in 2009, some financial journalists characterized the business as a pension plan funded by an automobile operation.

Shifting Responsibility

Companies addressed the dilemma by replacing defined benefit pension plans with defined contribution plans, like 401(k)s, where the companies contribute by matching employee contributions up to a certain percentage of the employee's salary. Defined contribution plans shield the company from future risk. The retirement savings burden shifts to the employee. Workers can save as much as they want, but once they are separated from the firm, the employer has no more risk or responsibility associated with their retirement.

Defined contribution plans serve to illustrate that we don't save enough. The idea of setting up a retirement plan from the moment you're employed makes wonderful sense due to the power of compounding returns on savings over time. But when you start working you might not earn enough to put something aside. Getting started can be challenging.

Additionally, a large part of the population doesn't save at all. The many and advantageous options offered by the retirement investment plan community aren't meaningful for those struggling to pay their current expenses. Consequently retirement for them is unrealistic, an unfortunate circumstance for increasingly more people in the United States. You might be getting Social Security in your sixties, but it's not enough to support a work-free retirement. As a result, many people work well past the age they thought they'd retire. For those who don't or can't, and for those who haven't saved anything or haven't saved enough, the golden years look less golden. It is something to think about as a nation as we face a continuously aging population.

A final note: Since its inception, economics has been called "the dismal science," which makes our last point of this final chapter an appropriate way to end our manuscript.

Takeaways

- Social Security was instituted in 1937 as a backstop for people living unusually long lives. The retirement age was 65, but average life expectancy was less.
- Funding for defined benefits plans proved inadequate to cover the burdens of an aging retired workforce living longer than the plans' actuaries expected.
- Pension obligations bankrupted some firms.
- Defined contribution plans shield sponsor companies from the risk of running out of money to fund the plans, as the retirement savings burden shifts to the employee.
- The plight of those who don't or can't work past retirement age and those who haven't saved anything or haven't saved enough is something to think about as a nation as we face a continuously aging population.

Equilibrium

The problem of saving for retirement is a good example of equilibrium in a larger sense, how it applies to how we should behave. If we work half our life and want a constant standard of living over our life, we should limit ourselves to consuming about half of what we make while working and save the other half for when we aren't. There are complications to the formula, but the stark reality behind the simple arithmetic is a lesson about something we should do, even if we don't or can't.

Epilogue

A few thoughts about economics, economists, and this book:

One: While outlier theories are more interesting, the consensus view is more accurate.

If you take the forecasts of a group of competent professional economists and somehow combine their forecasts, that combined forecast will, over time, be more accurate than any single one of the forecasts. Blue Chip, probably the most prominent of the consensus forecasts, combines dozens of individual forecasts. The outlooks of each of the twelve Federal Reserve regional banks and the Board of Governors are combined into the Fed's quarterly economic projections. The point is: If you try to do economic forecasting, it is very hard to beat the consensus.

Two: The strength of the consensus forecast is a problem for macroeconomists.

If you're trying to make a living doing macroeconomic forecasting and you are producing accurate forecasts, it's hard to attract attention because your forecast is going to look a lot like the consensus. If you appear on TV and say, "My forecast is close to what you've already heard," you won't be invited back. On the other hand, if you're an outlier, that is, you take an extreme position or offer consistently very upbeat or downbeat forecasts, you might get a lot of attention. You will be wrong most of the time, but eventually the economy will do something weird and you can say, "I told you so."

The strength of the consensus view also poses a problem when you are called upon to comment on the economy. The media devotes a considerable amount of time and space to contrarian forecasts. As a result, queries from your audiences are often based on alarmist suppositions that questioners might not realize are fringe positions, leaving you in the unenviable position of spending your time disabusing a questioner of those outlier beliefs.

Three: This text is intentionally mainstream.

One of the challenges to writing a book like this is deciding what to leave out. We employ a multitude of qualifiers: "usually," "often," "typically," "many," and "most." To every principle, there are exceptions. The economics profession generally has a good understanding of how and why those exceptions work, but presenting all the alternatives would be inordinately burdensome, to reader as well as writer, and wouldn't contribute substantially to understanding those principles.

Exceptions and alternatives to basic principles can ultimately serve to provide a deeper understanding of many of the subtleties and oddities that we see in everyday life. But they can be frustrating. As Harry Truman famously said, "Give me a one-handed economist. All my economists say 'on the one hand...' and then 'but on the other...'" There is a great deal of truth in Truman's complaint. Almost everything we say has to be qualified.

Four: Equilibrium is one of the most important concepts an economist can bring to a discussion.

Economic agents all over the world are trying to maximize their returns given their efforts, resources, and opportunities. They come together in markets that ultimately allocate goods and services among the many competing interests. We can readily see how the individual markets behave; it's more difficult, but exponentially more important, to recognize the general equilibrium across all markets. Disturbances in one market have implications for others. These interrelationships are particularly important to understand when policy changes are being considered where actions in one market will impose changes on other markets, and not always in obvious or pleasant ways. Understanding how general equilibrium works is key both for policy makers and everyone involved in any of the affected markets.

Businesspeople actively engaged in their particular markets rarely have an opportunity to get a larger view. They appreciate new information, but what I wanted most to convey in those many speeches I have delivered over the years is an understanding of how all markets fit together, and how we as individuals fit into that bigger picture.

Five: Timing is an issue.

Mike Shaw and I started thinking about this project in 2019. Since then COVID-19 has severely disrupted the U.S. and global economies. The resulting recession was not due to some economic problem that needed to be addressed. The U.S. economy was doing well. Fundamentals weren't a problem. And as the pandemic is resolved, the underlying economy will re-emerge, and growth and commerce will continue much as it did pre-COVID.

Of course, things will be different. Many underlying long-term trends were accelerated by the disruption, like the trend toward working remotely and the shift from brick-and-mortar to online retail. These changes will impact the workforce of the future, but most were going to happen anyway, and in the foreseeable future. The future simply came sooner than we anticipated.

I believe the long-run outlook for the U.S. economy is good. We've always faced challenges, and always will, from human error as well as the forces of nature, but fundamentally our economy is sound. Large parts of the world are experiencing rapid income growth, and we're better off with higher income neighbors and trading partners. The distribution of the benefits of our growth has been uneven, but addressing the underlying issues has gained some urgency and will contribute to an environment of good, sustainable, growth. I'm optimistic.

Thomas J. Cunningham
December 15, 2020

Glossary of Terms

Classes on the principles of economics are to a substantial degree vocabulary courses. You learn specific definitions of terms you are already vaguely familiar with and by doing so can draw inferences and distinctions that are not otherwise possible. The following terms are listed in the order they appear in the text:

Automatic Stabilizers: Government policies in place that act to stabilize the economy that do not require a specific act on the part of government to be effective. For example, progressive income tax rates increase tax burdens when incomes rise, and decrease tax burdens when incomes decline, allowing consumption to be smoother than the variations in income that support it.

Compensation Principle: The concept that whenever a policy is changed and there are winners and losers, and the gains enjoyed by the winners are greater than the losses suffered by the losers, it is possible for the winners to compensate the losers to be as well off as they were before the change. In practice, it is hard to make the principle work, but it is often the case that gains from changes are small but very widespread while the losses are concentrated in a few individuals. The gains are much larger than the losses, but not nearly as visible as the losses.

Derivative Security: A security that "derives" its value from another security rather than some fundamental underlying activity.

Diminishing Marginal Returns: The idea that as you use more of a good or service, the value from each additional unit declines. For example, as a firm adds workers each worker will add value to the output of the firm, but less value than the worker added before him or her.

Dynamic Instability: Any dynamic system that, as it adjusts over time, does not move toward a stable outcome. Consumer confidence, for example: If it falls, it will lead to lower consumption, which will lead to lower employment, which will cause a further decline in consumer confidence.

Economic Indicators: Measures that have broad implications about the condition of the macroeconomy. The unemployment rate, for example, reflects conditions in the labor market, which, in turn, reflects businesses' eagerness to employ and consumers' eagerness to purchase what businesses produce. Housing starts tell us not just about the housing construction market, but also about the durable and nondurable goods that go into a new house, along with providing some signal about the potential demand for new houses.

Emerging Market: A developing economy, frequently with low but rising per-capita income.

Equilibrium: An interaction of competing interests that produces a stable result. For example, suppliers will sell more but only at an increasing price. Consumers will demand more, but only a decreasing price. The equilibrium in the market is the unique price and quantity where the two segments of the market match.

Free Trade: Trade between economies that is unrestricted by external (usually governmental) forces; the free exchange between two willing parties.

Frictional Unemployment: The unemployment that is inevitable in a large economy due to "frictions" in the labor market, like workers being in the wrong location or with the wrong skills. It may be transitory for any individual, but in aggregate there will always be some small share of the labor force in this circumstance.

Fungible: Easily moved or transferred.

Great Recession: The period of December 2007 to June 2009; the longest recession in postwar U.S. history.

Gross Domestic Product (GDP) Accounts: The approach to accounting for economic activity. Often referred to as the National Income and Product Accounts, it is the summation of the real and nominal activity in the economy, broken down in detail by the sector doing that activity.

Home Country Bias: The tendency for people to invest in their own country even though they might generate better returns elsewhere.

Inside and Outside Lags: A measure of time it takes for policy to affect the economy. Inside lags are the time it takes the government to do something, that is, recognize there is a problem and then make some policy move to address it. Outside lags are the time it takes for that policy, once in place, to have an impact on the economy.

Inverted Yield Curve: A graphic line plotted sloping downward indicating longer-term interest rates are lower than short-term interest rates. It means markets believe interest rates will be lower in the future, which is typically associated with an expectation of an economic slowdown or recession.

Leading Economy: A relatively high per-capita income economy that is so because it is employing technologically advanced physical and human capital.

Long-Term Utility: A measure of well-being, a concept dating back to Jeremy Bentham and the Utilitarians. It is well-being in a broad sense: you, your health, your income, that of your family, society, whatever you think is important. Long-term utility takes a long-run view, for example, taking a job that pays less but provides a higher overall utility because is it in a better location for your family.

Macroeconomy: The entire economy. The distinction in economics is between macroeconomics, which studies how economies behave, and microeconomics, which studies how individual agents and markets in the economy behave. We typically use the term in reference to a country's economy; when we refer to the global economy, we often use the phrase "open-economy macroeconomics."

National Income Accounts: The bookkeeping system of the GDP accounts.

Negative Externalities: Bad things that happen as a consequence of some act with the cost of that bad thing not considered in the cost of the original action; for example, air pollution from mechanical processes that creates health and environmental costs that are not borne by the polluter.

Nominal GDP: What real GDP costs in money terms; all the goods and services produced priced in current dollar terms.

Political Economy: Another name for economics, applied in the eighteenth century when the discipline was new. The term "economics" started to replace "political economy" in the nineteenth century.

Primary Deficit: The deficit without considering debt service. It is an important calculation because debt service is an obligation the current government inherits from past decisions and, unless they are going to default on the debt, must be honored. A current government determines the primary deficit through the difference between current program spending and current tax revenue.

Real GDP: The actual quantity of goods and services, the tangible and intangible, produced by the economy. It is not affected by prices. It is usually expressed as the quantity of final goods and services consumed so as to avoid double counting of intermediate inputs that would be counted again in the final product.

Real Investment: The real additions to the physical or intellectual capital stock, for example, equipment on a factory floor. A financial transaction facilitates the addition to the capital stock, but it is the added equipment that is the real investment.

Reported Deficit: The primary deficit plus debt service. It is the amount the government must borrow. If the debt service is small, the reported and primary deficits are similar. But if the debt service is large, the reported deficit may be large even if the primary budget is in surplus.

Socially Responsible Investing: Investing with a goal of maximizing something more than just nominal return; usually investing in a firm that does something the investor believes is a good thing for society.

Sun Belt: The belt of Southern states that stretches across the continental United States; so called because those states generally have warmer climates than Northern states.

The Fisher Equation: A formula demonstrating that the nominal rate of interest equals the real return on investment plus expected inflation. The effect was first described by Irving Fisher.

Time Inconsistent Preferences: The concept that the "best" thing to do today may not be the best thing to do in the long run, that something that would give us utility today might be destructive if repeated. If we decide to do it today, we swear to never do it again. But then tomorrow we do it again and swear to never do it thereafter. On and on. The preferences for that choice are inconsistent over time.

Twin-Deficits Argument: The contention that the government's fiscal deficit is at least partly responsible for the balance of trade deficit, so an increase or decrease in the fiscal deficit will drive a similar move in the trade deficit.

Unintended (Unexpected) Inventory Investment: A buildup of inventories that was not intended by the producer. When production outpaces consumption in a way not expected by the producer, production will likely decline, as opposed to an intended buildup in inventories planned by the producer to meet a future increase in demand for the product.

Yield Curve: The relationship between the rate of return on bonds and their time to maturity. At any point in time there are a variety of bonds of varying lengths trading in the market. A bond that matures in one month will have a certain interest rate, one that matures in a year, another rate, one that matures in ten years another rate. Plotting the relationship between the maturing of the bond and its interest rate gives us the yield curve. It typically slopes upward because longer-term commitments usually require a higher rate of return.

About the Authors

Thomas J. Cunningham, PhD

Dr. Cunningham was the Chief Economist and Senior Vice President at the Metro Atlanta Chamber (MAC). He joined the MAC after retiring as Vice President, Senior Economist and Regional Executive of the Federal Reserve Bank of Atlanta.

During his thirty-year career with the Atlanta Fed, Tom was:

- Associate Director of Research; Interim Director of Research
- Vice President for the Regional Group, including responsibility for the Latin American Group
- Acting head of the Finance Group
- On the Bank's Personnel, Information Technology, and Risk Management committees
- A member of the Federal Reserve System's Information Security Group and Technology Services Council
- Acting Director of the Bank's Center for Real Estate Analytics, which he helped establish
- Author of many scholarly papers

His duties for the MAC included managing the research staff and assessing data for the Economic Development and Public Policy teams.

A native of Reedley, California, Tom received his bachelor's degree in economics, summa cum laude, from California State University, Fresno. He earned his MA, M. Phil., and PhD in economics from Columbia University. He taught economics at Barnard College and as an adjunct instructor at Iona College, Agnes Scott College, and Emory University. He attended the executive development program at the University of Pennsylvania's Wharton School and is a member of Leadership Atlanta's class of 2018.

Dr. Cunningham served as a board member of Atlanta's Neighborhood Nexus as well as the Georgia Intellectual Property Alliance. He was a member of the American Economic Association, the Western Economic Association and the Southern Economic Association.

Mike Shaw

Mike Shaw has been writing about and for businesses for more than five decades. He counts more than 15,000 published articles, from investigative pieces adapted by *60 Minutes* and *ABC 20/20*, to ghostwritten articles, white papers, blogs, and two books: *An Entrepreneurial Adventure* on the fiftieth anniversary of Healthdyne Corporation and *The Barn at Sandy Creek* about the quest to find, move, and reconstruct an antique barn as the centerpiece of a family estate.

In the 1970s, he created and edited *Mobile*, the Alabama city's first lifestyle magazine, and served as editor of industry-specific publications, including *Marina Magazine*, and *Play Meter Magazine*, the leading publication on coin-operated amusements, including the first video games.

Mike founded and has run three Atlanta-based marketing agencies. In the early 1980s, the first of his marketing firms introduced the concept of using corporate-sponsored publications to establish thought leadership. He and his team wrote and produced custom publications for multiple Fortune 50 companies. After selling the firm in 1990, he turned his attention to small and midsized health care, technology, and financial services firms, developing content to grow their businesses and enhance their competitiveness.

Mike's debut novel, *The Musician*, published by Blue Room Books, is scheduled for a 2021 debut. Mike holds an M.A. in English from the University of Miami.

Index